Linguistics and Law

Linguistics and Law offers a clear and concise introduction to making sense of the law through linguistics. Drawing on lexical semantics, syntax, and pragmatics to interpret both written and spoken laws, this book:

- addresses how to interpret legal documents such as contracts, statutes, constitutional provisions, and trademarks;
- provides thorough analyses of "language crimes" including solicitation, perjury, defamation, and conspiracy, as well as talk between police and criminal suspects;
- analyzes the *Miranda* warning in depth;
- tackles the question of whether there is a "language" of the law;
- draws on real-life case studies to aid understanding.

Written in an approachable, conversational style and aimed at undergraduate students with little or no prior knowledge of linguistics or law, this book is essential reading for those approaching this topic for the first time.

Jeffrey P. Kaplan is Professor of Linguistics at San Diego State University, USA, and a research associate affiliated with the linguistics program at Western Washington University, USA.

Routledge Guides to Linguistics

Series editor: Betty J. Birner is a Professor of Linguistics and Cognitive Science in the Department of English at Northern Illinois University.

Routledge Guides to Linguistics are a set of concise and accessible guidebooks which provide an overview of the fundamental principles of a subject area in a jargon-free and undaunting format. Designed for students of Linguistics who are approaching a particular topic for the first time, or students who are considering studying linguistics and are eager to find out more about it, these books will both introduce the essentials of a subject and provide an ideal springboard for further study.

This series is published in conjunction with the Linguistic Society of America. Founded in 1924 to advance the scientific study of language, the LSA plays a critical role in supporting and disseminating linguistic scholarship both to professional linguists and to the general public.

Titles in this series:

Why Study Linguistics
Kristin Denham and Anne Lobeck

Sign Languages
Structures and Contexts
Joseph C. Hill, Diane C. Lillo-Martin, and Sandra K. Wood

Language, Gender, and Sexuality
An Introduction
Scott F. Kiesling

More information about this series can be found at www.routledge.com/series/RGL

Linguistic Society of America

Linguistics and Law

Jeffrey P. Kaplan

Routledge
Taylor & Francis Group

LONDON AND NEW YORK

First published 2020
by Routledge
2 Park Square, Milton Park, Abingdon, Oxon OX14 4RN

and by Routledge
52 Vanderbilt Avenue, New York, NY 10017

Routledge is an imprint of the Taylor & Francis Group, an informa business

British Library Cataloguing-in-Publication Data
A catalogue record for this book is available from the British Library

Library of Congress Cataloging-in-Publication Data
Names: Kaplan, Jeffrey P., 1943– author.
Title: Linguistics and law / Jeffrey P. Kaplan.
Description: London ; New York, NY : Routledge, 2019. |
Series: Routledge guides to linguistics |
Includes bibliographical references and index.
Identifiers: LCCN 2019011594 | ISBN 9781138326132 (hardback) |
ISBN 9781138326156 (pbk.) | ISBN 9780429450020 (e-book)
Subjects: LCSH: Law–United States.–Language. |
Law–United States–Interpretation and construction |
Forensic linguistics–United States.
Classification: LCC KF380 .K37 2019 | DDC 340/.14–dc23
LC record available at https://lccn.loc.gov/2019011594

ISBN: 978-1-138-32613-2 (hbk)
ISBN: 978-1-138-32615-6 (pbk)
ISBN: 978-0-429-45002-0 (ebk)

Typeset in Times New Roman
by Newgen Publishing UK

Contents

Acknowledgments

Big thanks to Andrew Barker, undergraduate linguistics major at Western Washington University, for extensive and extremely valuable assistance with spectrograms.

Even bigger thanks to the series editor, Betty J. ("B-dot") Birner, for giving me the opportunity to write this book and for exact and insightful editorial suggestions, many of which I considered seriously.

I owe my beloved spouse Peri L. Good more than words can encode, not least for putting up with my absence, way too much, from interactions with her during the gestation of this book. I thank her too for precise and helpful editorial suggestions. And for listening, for the cookies, and for the laughs.

Thanks, PLG.

If any errors have slipped through, they are entirely on me.

Chapter 1

Introduction

1.1 What this book is about

Imagine being arrested. You are given the *Miranda* warning: "You have the right to remain silent. Anything you say can and will be used against you in a court of law..." In this quintessentially adversarial situation, you are told not only that silence is permissible but also that saying anything is likely to put you in legal jeopardy. Why would anyone under arrest say anything? But they do. A large majority of people arrested waive their right to silence, with estimates ranging from 78% to 96% (Wrightsman & Pitman 2010:157).

Imagine a less scary situation: you've been pulled over by a police officer. Maybe you've been speeding. After you have shown the officer your license, registration, and insurance card (what a relief that you remembered to put the insurance card in the glove compartment), the officer nicely says the following: "Do you mind if I look in your trunk?" Should you take this as a courteously worded command which must be obeyed, or a polite request for permission which can be refused?

In important areas, law is deeply linguistic. Not only are most laws written, in statutes and constitutions; also encoded in written language are the obligations and rights represented in contracts and wills. Most of the time, laws, contracts, and wills work fine, doing what they are intended to. But despite authors' best efforts, sometimes these legally operative texts have to be interpreted by courts, because unforeseen situations have arisen that the texts don't account for.

How can linguistics, the science of language, help us understand such things, and even help courts deal with them? That's what this book is about.

In Chapter 2, we'll use the lens of linguistics to help make sense of what happens when a person is "detained" or arrested by police. Police can detain you, without arresting you, for a variety of reasons: They may think you have committed an "infraction" such as speeding, or that you can provide information relevant to a criminal investigation. The police can ask you anything they want. In some places in the United States, you are required to answer (truthfully!) what your name is, but nowhere in the US do you have to answer much more than that, if anything at all. The police might want to search you or your car. If they don't have a search warrant (as they almost never do, in a detainment), they need to get your permission. There are exceptions. For instance, if they suspect you might have a weapon, they can pat you down, whether you like it or not. The police know all this. Few detainees do. The police use smart conversational moves to try to get you to answer questions or consent to a search. In this chapter, we'll look at the linguistics of police–detainee conversation.

If police have "probable cause" to believe you have committed a crime, they can arrest you. Obviously, this is much more serious than just being detained. If you are arrested, the police have to give you the *Miranda* warning. In Chapter 3 we'll look at the warning and issues around it. Specifically:

- the linguistics of the language of the warning;
- the sometimes-fuzzy distinction between free and compelled confessions;
- "speech acts" by arrestees (such as requests for an attorney);
- how courts have found arrested individuals to have waived *Miranda* rights; and
- how *Miranda* has been whittled away by Supreme Court decisions.

Chapter 4 will look at the difficulties involved in understanding surreptitiously recorded conversations, for example those made when a police agent wears a wire. Such recordings can be hard to understand, because of background noise, overtalking, and the fragmented nature of conversation. These problems can give rise to misperceptions due to listener expectations or bias. Linguistic analysis can sometimes help interpret such hard-to-understand recordings. Relevant areas include phonetics (how speech sounds are produced, and the structure of the sound waves of speech), phonology (organized patterning of speech sounds), and dialectology (regional and social differences in speech). These fields can help make clear what words were said. What speakers intended to communicate can be addressed by discourse analysis and pragmatics (how what is communicated can differ from what a person literally says).

Chapter 5 will look at the linguistics of four different categories of language crimes and other wrongful acts: perjury (lying under oath about something important), a violation against the judicial system; defamation, a violation against a person (and not a crime, but a **tort**, something that one can be sued for); solicitation of a crime, a violation against society; and conspiracy to commit a crime, another violation against society.

Chapter 6, on the "language" of the law, will look at the words used by lawyers and the syntax of lawyerly sentences.

Chapters 7 and 8 deal with interpreting legal documents like contracts and laws enacted by government. If an operative legal document – one that *does* something binding – is hard to understand or ambiguous, or seems to do the "wrong" thing, how do – and should – courts handle this interpretive problem? Problems can involve word meaning (lexical semantics) and the syntactic structure of sentences. And there's a logically prior question: Suppose what a contract or statute (a formally enacted law) says is different from the intent or purpose behind it. Should the actual language prevail, or the intent or purpose?

Chapter 9 will consider trademark law and how linguistics can help resolve, or at least help us understand, trademark disputes. Trademarks are symbols of businesses. Mostly they're linguistic: words and phrases, often names, like "Gillette," "McDonald's," and "Sony." Not always; images and physical forms, like McDonald's' golden arches, can be trademarks. Sometimes the issue in a trademark dispute is how similar sounding a new trademark is to an existing one. Phonetics and phonology can help. Lexical semantics can address how similar in meaning two competing trademarks are. Trademark fights can also be about whether a trademark word has, as a paradoxical price of business success, become widely used to refer to a thing without reference to its corporate ownership, and to other similar products or services. Examples: "xerox," "kleenex," "band-aid," "cellophane," and "frisbee." Here, grammar can help: Has the trademark become a common, rather than proper, noun, or even a verb?

Chapter 10 will summarize and look to the future.

1.2 The US judicial system

1.2.1 Courts

There are two main categories of courts in the US, the federal system and 50 state systems. Basically, the federal courts deal with federal laws and the state courts with state laws. Each system has trial courts and appellate courts, where a losing party at trial can appeal. Big exception: In a criminal case, the prosecution can't appeal a trial verdict of not guilty. Under certain circumstances, a losing party in a state system can appeal to the federal system. The federal system has two appellate levels, namely 13 circuit courts of appeal (so-named because in the nineteenth century judges "rode circuit" to hear cases, traveling by horseback to different locations), and the Supreme Court, which is the final arbiter of "what the law is."

1.2.2 Types of cases

Our system is adversarial. The idea is that the battle between two sides, each making its best argument from evidence and law, will tend to produce truth, as decided by a neutral fact-finder, a jury or judge. In a criminal case, the defendant, charged with committing a crime, is opposed by the government, represented by a prosecuting attorney. In jury trials, jury unanimity is required for conviction, using the high standard of belief by jurors that the defendant is guilty "beyond a reasonable doubt." If the defendant is found guilty, the state will impose punishment, almost always imprisonment for a period of time. In a civil case, the defendant has been accused by the **plaintiff** of having committed a **tort** (a "civil wrong"). The standard of proof is much lower than in criminal cases, **preponderance of the evidence**, that is, the defendant is more likely than not to be responsible for the harm to the plaintiff. Most commonly, if the plaintiff wins, the defendant has to pay the plaintiff money ("**damages**"). A winning plaintiff can be awarded **compensatory** damages, for costs like medical expenses or harm to property incurred because of the defendant's tort, and sometimes **punitive** damages, when the fact-finder (judge or jury) wants to punish the defendant for egregious behavior.

1.3 What this book is not about

1.3.1 A broad area: language and law

Linguistics and law is part of a broader field of "language and law," which includes topics like legal interpreting; communication in legal contexts with speakers of minority languages, and with children; and laws governing language rights of linguistic minorities and policies of language planning, including educational programs like bilingual education and English as a second language. Few countries are truly monolingual, and many have large populations speaking different languages. There is a range of ways countries use law to address issues arising from the use of different languages. This fascinating area will not be addressed.

1.3.2 Author identification

Sometimes linguists consult to attorneys to provide evidence on whether some particular individual authored a certain document, or to provide evidence against that conclusion. When they do, they adduce linguistic facts, for example, occurrence of unusual word collocations, punctuation or capitalization patterns, or other possible linguistic giveaways as to identity or non-identity. Such work contributed to the resolution of the "Unabomber" case of the 1970s, 80s, and 90s. Despite the appeal of using linguistic analysis to determine authorship, there are problems, which have deterred some linguists from undertaking such work. To provide scientific evidence for author identification (or non-identification), the procedures used must be precisely stated and replicable, not just anecdotal. Replicability requires a large quantity of data, ideally lots of texts produced by a suspect author and lots of texts produced by others that are on some well-defined basis comparable. It can be hard to reach or even approach this ideal, making it hard to apply sophisticated statistical tools to provide quantified evidence. This area is complex enough to make doing justice to the various controversial parts of it impossible in a book of this length.

1.4 Who this book is for, and what background is assumed

This book is primarily intended for undergraduates with no background in either linguistics or law but interest in both. You'll get introduced to the areas of both that you'll need as the need arises in the chapters that follow, with a bit of an introduction below to topics in semantics and pragmatics that will be particularly important. And the Appendix has an introduction to phonetics and phonology, which, if you have no background in linguistics, you'll need for Chapter 4.

In the area of semantics, the **denotation** of an expression is the set of its possible **referents**. The referent of an expression is what a speaker uses the expression to refer to – something in the world. If I tell you "President Trump's hand looked tiny," the referent of the expression *President Trump's hand* in that expression is – ready for it? – President Trump's hand. Common nouns – *hand, car, escalator, ladder* – have vast numbers of possible referents. But none of those words has a referent until it's used in an actual utterance.

What it has is a denotation, the set of (for example) hands, past, present, future, imagined, imaginable, unimaginable but possible. Common nouns, and all words except grammatical-function words such as conjunctions (like *and* and *or*) and determiners (like *a* and *the*), also have **senses**, which are basically "meanings," which you can learn from a dictionary definition or an example ("That's a ladder," "That's red").

Proper nouns – names – don't have senses, just referents. *Iowa* means that state. *Benjamin Franklin* means that guy. *New York* means that city, or state; the apparent adjective and the name of an English city is irrelevant to the meaning of *New York* today.

Pragmatics is about context-sensitive meaning. The two areas of pragmatics that will be important in this book are **speech act theory** and **Gricean implicature**. Speech act theory is about things speakers do with language: assert, ask, thank, congratulate, promise, warn, appoint, christen, and others, but not sew or admire. Not surprisingly, asserting, etc., are called speech acts.

Gricean implicature is so named because of its originator, the British philosopher of language Paul Grice (1975). **Implicatures** are strongly invited inferences, reasoned conclusions about what a speaker meant to communicate. The reasoning is based on what a speaker literally said, the context of utterance, and some presumably universal expectations people have about human communication. Example: If you tell me your friend Jane has two children, you invite me to infer (that is, you **implicate**) that Jane has *exactly* two children, even though she could have three or more without your having technically lied; if Jane has three or more children, she has two, which is what you said. You *misled* me, but you didn't actually lie, by implicating exactly two. The implicature arises based on the assumption that speakers are expected to provide enough information for the current communicative purposes. If Jane has children but I don't know how many, and you tell me she has two, I expect and assume that you have obeyed the "Maxim of Quantity," this expectation about providing enough information. If Jane had three children, not just two, you presumably would have said so, and because you didn't, but instead said that she had two, I infer that you intended me to understand that she has exactly two.

The Maxim of Quantity is one of just a few Gricean maxims. Other important ones are the Maxims of **Quality** and **Relevance** (technically called by Grice "**Relation**"). Quality is about truth and having evidence, the expectation that speakers try not to say untrue things and not assert things they don't have evidence for. You can see the power of the "having evidence" part from the following example: You're married. An acquaintance tells you "Your spouse is faithful to you." (*Whoa!*) The Maxim of Relevance is about – guess what – being relevant. You can see its operation in its apparent violation. Suppose you say "Professor Bee is an old bag with bad breath," and your interlocutor replies "The capital of Uganda is Kampala, isn't it?" Irrelevant! Actually, however, your conversational partner might be speaking relevantly, by signaling that the topic you raised is inappropriate. Maybe the odious Professor Bee happens to be standing behind you. Just about all utterances are made with the intent that they'll be relevant, and the generality and power of the Relevance maxim can be seen in the fact that addressees just about always seek relevance in whatever they are told, even if that relevance is not obvious right away.

A phenomenon that straddles the line between semantics and pragmatics is **presupposition**. A presupposition of an utterance is whatever the speaker takes to be part of the common ground of background knowledge shared with the addressee which is necessary for the utterance to make sense. For example, *Where did you put my keys?* presupposes that the addressee put the speaker's keys somewhere. *Mary stopped beating her husband* presupposes that (i) Mary had a husband and (ii) she had been beating him. Certain grammatical structures, called presupposition **triggers**, automatically presuppose. Sentences with *wh*-words (*where, when, who, what, which, why*, and, yes, *how*) are presupposition triggers. Asking a person why – or where, or when, or with whom, or how – a person did such-and-such presupposes that the person did it. Definite noun phrases are another presupposition trigger; the presupposition is that the referent of the noun phrase exists. Contrast *Seeing the ghost would be scary* with *Seeing a ghost would be scary.*

1.5 Citation

1.5.1 Cases

In the following chapters, court cases will be cited, mostly US Supreme Court cases, but also cases from circuit courts of appeal, and even a few trial cases. Case opinions are printed in books called "Reports" or "Reporters." They're also available online. Citations to these opinions have a standard format. Example: *Miranda v. Arizona*, 384 U.S. 436 (1966). In this, the first part names the parties (*Miranda* and the state of Arizona); the next part identifies the number of the report volume (384); next, the letters "U.S." stand for "United States Reports," which is the name of the official volumes of Supreme Court cases; next comes the page where the case opinion begins (436); and finally there is the year of the decision (1966). When a cite is to a particular page in an opinion, that page number follows the page number where the opinion begins, like this: *Miranda v. Arizona*, 384 U.S. 436, 444 (1966), in which "444" indicates the particular page cited to. Because all cases cited in this book are available online, where specific page numbers are not always identified, citations in this book to specific pages in opinions will not always be provided.

Some citations are to an unofficial Supreme Court reporter, such as the Supreme Court Reporter. Cites to this reporter have the same elements as cites to United States Reports, but since the former is a different series of books from the latter, it has different volume and page numbers. Here's the Supreme Court Reporter cite to *Miranda: Miranda v. Arizona*, 86 S. Ct. 1062 (1966).

There is no official reporter for circuit court of appeals cases. Opinions are printed in reporters published by a private company, West Publishing. Cites to appellate opinions published by West have a similar array of information as for Supreme Court cases: the names of the parties, the number of the volume in which the case appears, an abbreviation to one of the three series of volumes of West's "Federal Reporter," the first page of the opinion, the name of the court, and the year of the decision. Example: *Eagan v. Duckworth*, 843 F.2d 1554 (7th Cir. 1988). In this citation, "F.2d" means the second series of Federal Reporter volumes, which covers the years 1924–1993.

1.5.2 Statutes

Every jurisdiction has its own standard form for citing statutes. The federal perjury statute, which we'll meet in Chapter 5, is cited like this: 18 U.S.C. § 1621. In this, the first part, "18," identifies the area, or **title,** of law, in this case criminal law. "U.S.C." means "United States Code." Finally, the section, 1621. There are 53 titles. Here's a sample of other titles: the office of the President, including election rules (Title 3), domestic security (Title 6), bankruptcy (Title 11), the census (Title 13), commerce and trade (Title 15), copyright law (Title 17), internal revenue (Title 26), war and national defense (Title 50).

1.6 Linguistic notation

Common practice in linguistics is to stick a symbol in front of language items or sequences that are "wrong" one way or another. **Ungrammatical** ones are marked with an asterisk: *Ate go banana the, *She am here of was.* Items or sequences that are wrong semantically or don't fit contextually, but which are grammatical (and maybe fine in other contexts) are marked with a "#": #*Put the circular square inside the one-dimensional cube. #Colorless green ideas sleep furiously. Speaker A: Hi, how ya doin? Speaker B: #Kampala is the capital of Uganda.*

1.7 Boldfaced items

Boldfaced words in this book signal one or the other of the following: (i) They mark technical terms in either linguistics or law. If you don't know a boldfaced term or can't figure out its meaning from the explanation provided or the context, you should look it up. (ii) They advise you to read a particular case, an important one for the current context which space limitations preclude discussing.

Chapter 2

Detention and arrest

2.1 Detention

You've borrowed your brother's car and are driving it through town in the evening. Suddenly flashing red lights in your rear view mirror let you know you are being pulled over. Oops. Forgot to tell you: Your brother's not literally a crook as far as you know, but pretty disreputable and possessed of unsavory friends. Other than that, you have no reason to feel particularly afraid; let's say you're adult, male, white, and by appearance neat and middle class. (Things are different, if you're female or a person of color.) Being pulled over and given a ticket is an irritation, but nothing worse. But this time, you're nervous. After stopping, you retrieve your driver's license from your wallet. As a police officer approaches the passenger window, you roll it down and you fumble in the glove compartment for the car registration and insurance card. Thank goodness they're there. The officer utters the expected "May I see your license and registration?" You hand them to the officer. He inquires about the different names on your license and the registration. You explain. The officer asks if you know why he pulled you over. You don't, and you say so. The officer says something about a broken taillight. Now things get interesting. The policeman says "Do you mind if I look in the trunk?" In the next half a second or so you very quickly consider the following: Your brother could have left anything in the trunk, including illegal drugs, illegal weapons, possibly stolen goods. Probably not, but you're not sure. Obviously for the officer to look in the trunk could put you and your brother at risk. How should you reply to the police officer's polite words? If you say "Actually I do mind," what is likely to happen? Are the officer's words what they appear to be on the surface – a polite request which can be declined – or what the context suggests – a command which must be obeyed, clothed in polite form?

In such a situation, what would you do? In fact, people in such situations tend to say that it's OK for the cop to search even if they know there is something incriminating there. One reason is not knowing whether one has the right to say "Actually I do mind." Another is the awareness that to turn down the request will communicate guilt. Contrast saying "Go ahead," which communicates innocence by implying that you have nothing to hide, as well as cooperativeness and good citizenship. If you do have something in the trunk you wouldn't want the officer to see, maybe the officer won't find it or won't understand what it is.

To understand an encounter like this, two lines of exploration are needed, one into an area of linguistics called **speech act theory** and one into the law governing stops of citizens by police, **detentions**.

2.1.1 Speech act theory

Speech acts are acts that are carried out by speaking, like warning, thanking, promising, congratulating, pronouncing a couple married, asking, and – crucially here – requesting and ordering; but not baking, sneezing, or scratching your back.

Actually, only one type of speech act has this character of carrying out an act by means of words. (A little technical detour is needed here.) This kind is called **illocutionary**. Illocutionary acts are acts carried out by speaking that are intended to achieve some particular effect, called **perlocutionary**. Confused? Bear with me. There are three kinds of speech act, **locutionary,** illocutionary, and perlocutionary. Locutionary acts are acts *of* speaking, for example uttering a sequence of speech sounds. They're not all that interesting. Perlocutionary acts are acts achieved by successful executions of illocutionary acts or sequences of them: The perlocutionary act of persuading occurs when a speaker performs, say, a series of (illocutionary) acts of asserting, which together have the cognitive effect on the addressee of changing their mind – of getting them persuaded. Perlocutionary *acts* are usually better thought of as perlocutionary *effects*. Here are a few examples showing the relation between illocutionary acts and perlocutionary effects: The illocutionary act of promising is intended to have the perlocutionary effect of getting the addressee to recognize that the speaker has made a commitment to carry out a future act. The illocutionary act of pronouncing a couple married is intended to have the perlocutionary effect of making the couple married. The illocutionary effect of apologizing is intended to have the perlocutionary effect assuaging the addressee's ill feelings caused by a prior act by the speaker. Some illocutionary acts have their intended perlocutionary effect built in, as it were: among others, pronouncing a couple married, appointing, firing, and sentencing. Others don't: promises and apologies, for example, can be recognized as insincere, resulting in failure to achieve the intended perlocutionary effect.

In this chapter, and in fact the rest of this book, it will be mainly illocutionary acts that are of interest.

A useful taxonomy of illocutionary acts constructed by the philosopher of language John Searle (1976) divides them thusly:

I   Searle's taxonomy of speech acts

Representatives: Asserting, hypothesizing, suggesting, etc. The only category for which "true" or "false" applies to what is asserted, etc. The point is to position the speaker as believing in the truth of what is asserted, etc., to a greater or lesser strength depending on the particular speech act. (Asserting is stronger than guessing.)

Directives: Commanding, requesting, begging, inviting, etc. The point is to get the addressee to do something.

Commissives: Promising, threatening. The point is to commit the speaker to a future act.

Expressives: Thanking, congratulating, apologizing, welcoming, etc. The point is to express the speaker's emotions regarding an act, event, or situation involving the addressee.

Declarations: Appointing, pronouncing a couple married, sentencing, firing, christening, declaring war, and others. Declarations uniquely among these categories guarantee the achievement of the intended perlocutionary effect. (If you are officiating at a wedding, when you utter the words "I now pronounce you husband and wife," the happy couple becomes – suddenly – married.)

The rules for carrying out speech acts are usually characterized as **"felicity conditions"** (literally "happiness conditions"), i.e., the necessary and sufficient conditions for successful – felicitous (= "happy") – performance of these acts.

In our story, the police officer has asked if you mind if he looks in your trunk. What speech act has he performed, a question, a request, or a command? In this context, his utterance can't be functioning as a question, despite its form, and despite the forms of possible answers: "Yes, I do mind" and "No, I don't mind." The reason is that the speech act of asking is carried out to try to get information, but the officer is not curious about your feelings. Rather, he wants to search your trunk. In fact, in many contexts, "Do you mind…" is a conventional way to make a request ("Do you mind closing the window?"). Here, the cop clearly wants to look in your trunk, so this is either a request for your permission to do that, or, given his power over you, a command for you to open the trunk.

To understand the difference, consider the felicity conditions for both (the categories on the left of the table, adapted slightly from Searle 1969, are explained below):

[2]	Felicity conditions for requests	Felicity conditions for commands
Semantic content:	Future act by addressee	Future act by addressee

Preparatory conditions:	Speaker believes Addressee can carry out the future act	Speaker believes Addressee can carry out the future act
	It's not obvious that Addressee would carry out the act without being requested	It's not obvious that Addressee would carry out the act without being commanded
		Speaker and Addressee both believe that Speaker has the right to compel Addressee to carry out the act
Essence:	Counts as non-enforceable attempt to get addressee to carry out the act	Counts as enforceable attempt to get addressee to carry out the act

The **semantic content** is the meaning separated out from the speech act, in both cases here a future act by the addressee. In our story, the future act is complying with the request or order. Comparing other speech acts: The semantic content of a **warning** is simply a future event. (The assumed badness of the event for the addressee will be captured in the preparatory conditions.) The semantic content of the speech act of **thanking** is a past act by the addressee. The semantic content of the speech act of **asserting** is the content of what is asserted.

Preparatory conditions are whatever has to be true ahead of time for felicitous performance of the speech act. For both requests and commands, the preparatory conditions are the speaker's belief in the addressee's capacity to carry out the future act and the fact that it's not obvious that the addressee would carry out the act absent the request or command. (By the way, observe that the speaker's actual desire for the addressee to carry out the future act is not included, because people can request or order behavior that they don't really want. For example, a law or regulation might require them to order or request an action they personally do not want to occur.)

Where requests and commands differ is whether the speech participants believe that the speaker has the right to compel the addressee's compliance: Yes in commands, No in requests. This difference appears also in the difference in the two "essences," or what the speech act "is" or "counts as": a request can be refused, a command can be enforced.

Back to our story again. How can you tell whether the officer's words are a request, or a command?

One more element of speech act theory may help. Or not; stay tuned. It's important anyway for fully understanding the nature of interactions like the one we are pretending you are in, as well as others that will appear in this book. This element is the frequent **indirectness** of speech acts. A **direct** speech act is carried out unambiguously, in one of two ways. One is by use of the relevant speech act verb as in an utterance like "I *promise* to bring beer to your party," in which there is not only the speech act verb *promise,* but the first person pronoun *I* and the present tense form of the verb. Because that form just about guarantees that it is being used to perform a speech act, it's called **performative**. The other way is by use of a sentence form conventionally associated with a particular speech act. For the speech act of questioning, the conventional form is a sentence structure in which the positions of the subject and the auxiliary verb are reversed, as in *Can you open the trunk.* For the speech act of apologizing, the conventional form is the specific words "I'm sorry." Many speech acts are carried out indirectly, by performing one speech act in order to carry out another. Example: You've been invited to a dinner that you don't want to attend. You can carry out the speech act of declining the invitation by saying "I have to work on my linguistics paper," that is, by performing the speech act of **asserting**. Because both you and your interlocutor naturally expect relevance in communication, you know that your addressee will understand, from your words in the context, that you are turning down the invitation, even though you haven't explicitly said that.

Back again to our story. You know that the police officer isn't asking whether you mind his looking in your trunk out of curiosity about your feelings, the way a friend might ask you "Would you mind if somebody mispronounced your name?"; rather, you understand that the cop is doing his job, part of which apparently now includes looking in your trunk. So, by asking a factual Yes-or-No question, he has indirectly performed a speech act of requesting or of ordering. Because he is a police officer, guessing which speech act – a request or a command – he is performing may not be that hard. He did pull you over, and you know that's lawful; he did ask for your license and registration, and you know that's also lawful; and you also are aware that police sometimes search people's cars, presumably just as lawfully. So, you conclude, in the half second it takes you to process what is going on, that the cop's words are a politely worded command, so it is probably a good idea to let the officer look in your trunk. And even if the words weren't a command, why not convey innocence and cooperativeness while hoping your brother hasn't left the fruit of one of his friends' crimes in the trunk?

2.1.2 Law about detentions

Actually, if the only reason the officer pulled you over was because of a broken taillight, or because he had a faint suspicion that all was not right with your brother's car or with you (in this variant of the story, let's make you Hispanic or African-American), or because he needed to issue one more ticket to meet his quota for the day, or because he was bored, he has no right to look in your trunk – unless you give him permission. The Constitution's Fourth Amendment protects people from "unreasonable searches." Looking in your trunk would be a search; would it be "unreasonable?" The word *unreasonable* is a scalar adjective, like *tall, rich, smart,* and *interesting,* in contrast with non-scalar adjectives like *dead, male,* and *identical.* Scalar adjectives can be compared – *taller than, more interesting than* – but non-scalar ones can't, except as jokes or metaphors - #*deader than,* #*more identical than* are distinctly odd. So where on the unreasonableness scale does looking in your trunk fit?

Before we get to that, another detour is in order. The use of the word *unreasonable* in the Fourth Amendment is an example of the Constitution's purposeful vagueness. It's there in order to cover the unpredictable. Other vague protection are the Fifth and Fourteenth Amendments' guarantees of "due process," the Sixth Amendment's guarantee of a right to a "speedy" trial, and the Eighth Amendment's protection against "excessive" bail or fines and against "cruel and unusual" punishments.

It is worth noting here that law folks and linguists differ in their terminology for uncertainty of meaning. Law folks tend to use the term *ambiguous* for any uncertainty of meaning, and sometimes use *ambiguous* and *vague* interchangeably. Linguists distinguish sharply between **ambiguity** and **vagueness;** ambiguity means "having distinct meanings" and "**paraphrasable** in different ways that are not paraphrases of each other." Sentences that are paraphrases mean the same. So *The woman saw the girl with the telescope* is ambiguous between a meaning shown in the paraphrase *The woman used the telescope to see the girl* and one shown in the paraphrase *The woman saw the girl who had the telescope.* In contrast, vagueness means indeterminacy of meaning because of lack of specificity. A vague expression can be made more specific, but the more specific statement is not a paraphrase of the original, because it packs more meaning in. *The lawyer sat on the chair* is vague with respect to the kind of chair. A more specific statement might be *The lawyer sat on the armchair* or *...on the overstuffed red armchair* or *...on the sagging recliner,* etc. These are not paraphrases of *The lawyer sat on the chair.*

Back now to the law about searches. The "unreasonable search" part of the Fourth Amendment has been made more precise by Supreme Court decisions. A 1968 decision, *Terry v. Ohio,* permitted police searches of people they have stopped, that is, searches – patdowns – for weapons, the reason being to protect the safety of police officers. By implication, such searches were the only kind allowed, in stops that fell short of being arrests.

Traffic stops were later, in *Adams v. Williams* (1972), defined as "Terry stops" after the *Terry v. Ohio* decision, and *Adams v. Williams,* along with *Michigan v. Long* (1983), extended *Terry* to permit searches in cars, but only for weapons, and only if the police had good reason to suspect that weapons were present, for example if they had a tip from an informant. Without probable cause to believe that an actual crime had been committed (which would presumably lead to an arrest, not just a stop), no other basis for search was – and is – allowed. However, if, during a safety-oriented search for weapons, other bad things are found – for instance, illegal drugs or stolen goods – they can be used against the person stopped (*Michigan v. Long*).

So (back again to our story) you've been pulled over for a broken taillight in your borrowed car, but the police officer has no reason to suspect that you might have access to a weapon in the trunk. Maybe you're visibly nervous, and that might justify a policeman's suspicion that all is not right. The policeman might have ordered you to get out of your car; that's constitutional, to protect the safety of police (*Pennsylvania v. Mimms* (1977)), but the cop who stopped you didn't do that. (That would be a different story, although if the officer's words were "Do you mind stepping out of the car?" the same uncertainty might bedevil you as to whether you had received an order or just a request.) In our story, the officer just asked if you minded if he looked in the trunk. Unaware that you have the right to refuse, and hoping your brother hasn't left something bad in the trunk, you say to the waiting officer, "No, go ahead," and you pop the trunk. The officer goes around to the back of the car, lifts the trunk lid, and... disaster. He finds the bag of stolen jewelry your brother left there along with a bag of white powder that later turns out to be heroin, returns to the side of the car, orders you to step out of the car, has you turn around and place your arms up on the roof of the car, pats you down for weapons, instructs you to put your hands behind your back, locks cuffs on your wrists, tells you that you are under arrest for possession of stolen goods and of illegal drugs, and reads you the *Miranda* warning.

Later, your lawyer tells you that the search of the trunk may have been unlawful, in fact unconstitutional, because the officer had no reasonable basis to fear for his safety from a weapon in the trunk and you had not really consented to the search. If the search was unconstitutional, the jewels and heroin will be excluded from evidence, and you'll probably get off. Not only that, your brother probably won't face legal jeopardy either. But what about it: did you consent? On the surface it certainly looks like you did; the officer asked if you minded if he looked in the trunk; you replied "No, go ahead," and opened the trunk for him. To see if this super-ficially clear giving of consent really should be seen as consenting, let's look at the speech act of consenting.

2.1.3 Consenting

Here are the felicity conditions for consenting:

3   Felicity conditions for consenting

Semantic content:	Future act by addressee
Preparatory conditions:	(i) Addressee has the ability to carry out the future act.
	(ii) Addressee has proposed the future act.
	(iii) Speaker believes that Addressee has no right to perform the future act without speaker's permission.
	(iv) Speaker believes that Speaker is free to withhold permission.
Sincerity condition:	Speaker is genuinely willing for Addressee to carry out the future act.
Essence:	The utterance counts as Speaker's giving permission to Addressee to do the act.

Did you notice the inclusion of the sincerity condition? Look back at (2): there's no sincerity condition for requests or commands. The reason, as mentioned above, is that a person might issue a request or a command without sincerely wishing it to be obeyed. Perhaps some regulation required it. You can probably imagine other scenarios. But consenting is different. If a robber points a gun at you and says "I'm going to take your wallet now, OK?" and you say, to save your life, "OK," have you really consented? There are two aspects to this question and its answer. One is sincerity: Are you really willing for the robber to take your wallet? Of course you don't want him to, but if it's a binary choice and the alternative is being shot, yes you do. But now let's add the second aspect: the availability of a genuine option to withhold consent. This one is captured in the fourth preparatory condition in (3) above. Under most circumstances, being held up at gunpoint is being forced to do something, which is quite different from consenting to do it. There are contexts in which a person might actually choose to be shot rather than submit to a demand; imagine a secret agent who has been captured by the bad guys, and who has information it's important not to divulge, who makes a heroic choice for patriotic reasons. But common sense tells us that in most other contexts being threatened with death removes the possibility of true consent. Genuine consent seems to require not only sincerity but also the availability of a reasonable choice to withhold consent.

This has an interesting implication for the linguistic nature of consenting. The usual way to carry out a speech act unambiguously (or just about) is to use the performative structure "I (hereby) Verb..." (for instance, "I hereby promise to...," "I (hereby) resign...," "I (hereby) sentence you to..." But this form doesn't work to signal genuine consent. A person can grammatically say "I (hereby) consent to...," but if the consent is insincere, a true act of consenting has not occurred.

The needed availability, for true consenting. of the opportunity to withhold consent also means that apparent consenting to something which one is legally obligated to do isn't true consent. Imagine that our story is a little different: The officer orders you to step out of your car and then asks "Do you mind if I pat you down?" You don't have a concealed weapon on you, or any contraband, so you reply "OK." This might feel, to you, like consent, but in fact there's something wrong here, since the cop can lawfully pat you down whether you want him to or not. If you know that, your OKing the pat-down is not a true consenting. What if you don't know the relevant law? From your perspective, if you believe you can refuse, it is a valid consent. This is why the preparatory conditions (iii) and (iv) include "Speaker believes..." So the problem in the interaction is due to the officer: He implied to you, falsely, that you had a choice. Why would he do that? Most likely to put you at your ease, as much as possible in this context, in order to get you to do what he wants without making you feel unduly threatened, thereby both making his job easier and potentially opening the door to your acceding to additional requests, including some without the force of law behind them. **A good case to read at this point is *Bumper v. North Carolina*, 391 U. S. 543 (1968).**

2.1.4 Politeness theory

The relevant linguistics here is known as **politeness theory** (Brown and Levinson 1987). Politeness theory makes major use of the concept of **face**, which has two aspects: **Positive face** is the desire to be approved of; **negative face** is the desire not to be imposed on. When people interact, they protect not only their own face, but others' as well, possibly on the assumption that nice behavior toward others generates the same back (or maybe out of morality, an application of the golden rule). Both positive and negative face are involved in a police officer's seeking consent, positive face because being asked nicely makes one feel respected (contrast being roughly ordered), and – probably more importantly – negative face because any request, including a request for consent, is an imposition. One way to preserve an addressee's negative face is to give options, or at least pretend to. Obviously "Do you mind...?" and similar questions can have that effect.

2.1.5 Schneckloth v. Bustamonte

Let's return to our story. At a pre-trial hearing your lawyer argues that the jewels and heroin the police officer found in the trunk have to be excluded as evidence, as "fruit from a poisonous tree," that is, as product of an unconstitutional search, a violation of the Fourth Amendment's protection against unreasonable searches. Your lawyer argues that genuine consent requires that the person consenting must know that not consenting is a real option, and asserts correctly that you didn't know that. Unfortunately, it turns out that your lawyer is not very experienced in criminal matters, and has forgotten the holding in a 1973 Supreme Court case, *Schneckloth v. Bustamonte*, a case he probably studied in his Criminal Procedure class in law school, but that was way back in first year. Just as unfortunately, the prosecutor knows the case and shoots down your lawyer's argument by citing the holding in *Schneckloth*:

[4]   Voluntariness is a question of fact to be determined from all the circumstances, and while the subject's knowledge of a right to refuse is a factor to be taken into account, the prosecution is not required to demonstrate such knowledge as a prerequisite to establishing a voluntary consent.

Schneckloth v. Bustamonte, 412 U.S. 218, 248–249 (1973)

The majority in *Schneckloth* took the absence of explicit coercion as evidence of consent. According to the *Schneckloth* majority, the needs of law enforcement are paramount in a detainment situation; police work would be seriously hindered if the prosecution had to prove that a defendant knew they could refuse consent. Defendants could simply testify that they did not know that. Proving that they did would be nearly impossible.

Since *Schneckloth* is still good law, you lose! The jewels and heroin are admitted into evidence. Since this is a made-up story, we can give you a happy ending: Your brother has suddenly got religion and turns himself in, confesses to burglarizing a jewelry store and buying the heroin from someone with the intent to sell it, and testifies that as far as he knew you would have had no reason to believe anything bad was in the trunk. You get off, and your brother goes off to prison for a few years. There, he becomes a model prisoner and advocate for prison reform.

But what about consent, both in law and in linguistics? As far as law is concerned, *Schneckloth* is the law: a person can be taken to have consented to a search even without knowing that they had the right to withhold consent.

Three justices in *Schneckloth* dissented, valuing the Fourth Amendment's protection over law enforcement practicality, and arguing that genuine consent necessarily includes the consenter's knowledge that they have the right to refuse. This view fits the felicity conditions given in (3) above, which include the speaker's belief in the availability of a non-consent option.

Here's a bit of what Justice William O. Douglas wrote in dissent:

5   It wholly escapes me how our citizens can meaningfully be said to have waived something as precious as a constitutional guarantee without ever being aware of its existence. In my view, the Court's conclusion is supported neither by "linguistics," nor by "epistemology," nor, indeed, by "common sense."

> *Schneckloth v. Bustamonte*, 412 U.S. 218,
> 277 (1973) Douglas, J., dissenting

Accepting the soundness of the analysis of consenting offered above does not require the legal conclusion that the dissenting justices in *Schneckloth* reached. One can value practicality of law enforcement over semantics, and find catching criminals more important than applying the true nature of consenting in law enforcement.

2.2 Arrests and confessions

You've been arrested. Yikes, or, probably, a stronger epithet. To understand what goes on communicatively in this extremely scary context, it doesn't matter whether you're guilty or innocent. The police have **probable cause** (i.e., good reason) to believe that you have committed a crime. (Or at least they purport to, but we won't worry here about corrupt police behavior.) In fact, if you are ever arrested, one thing to bear in mind is that the police are not your friends; they believe you perpetrated a crime. Since catching criminals is their job, they'll do all they can to justify their belief that you are the "perp." One pretty sure way to do this is to get you to confess.

2.2.1 Getting confessions

The history of how confessions have been obtained is interesting. The first time a forced confession was overturned by the Supreme Court was in an 1897 case, *Bram v. United States*. In *Bram*, a suspect was forced to strip naked and was interrogated by a detective with no one else present. The defendant answered a question in a way that implied guilt – not an explicit confession, but close enough to count as one. The Supreme Court, citing the Fifth Amendment's protection against compelled self-incrimination ("No person... shall be compelled in any criminal case to be a witness against himself") along with the history behind it (and a lot more; it's a long opinion), threw out the confession on the grounds that it was compelled. Here is how the Court put it:

[6]   Bram had been brought ... to the office of the detective, and there, when alone with him, ... while he was in the act of being stripped, or had been stripped, of his clothing, was interrogated by the officer, who was thus, ... exercising complete authority and control over [him]. Although these facts may not, when isolated each from the other, be sufficient to warrant the inference that an influence compelling a statement had been exerted; yet, when taken as a whole, in conjunction with the nature of the communication made, they give room to the strongest inference that the statements of Bram were not made by one who... could be considered a free agent.

Bram v. United States, 168 U.S. 532,
564–565 (1897)

The *Bram* approach can be summarized as looking at the "totality of the circumstances" surrounding the confession to infer compulsion.

Bram was decided in 1897. It was a federal case because the crime was committed at sea rather than in a state. One reason it took so long after the founding of the nation to get to this point in the U.S. justice system was that in our federal system, most criminal cases are state, not federal matters, and the federal courts couldn't tell state courts how to handle evidentiary matters like confessions – that is, until after the Civil War, when the Fourteenth Amendment was ratified, with its guarantees of **due process** and **equal protection** of the laws explicitly applicable to the states. Here's Section 1 of the Amendment, in which those two guarantees are boldfaced:

[7]   All persons born or naturalized in the United States, and subject to the jurisdiction thereof, are citizens of the United States and of the State wherein they reside. No State shall make or enforce any law which shall abridge the privileges or immunities of citizens of the United States; **nor shall any State deprive any person of life, liberty, or property, without due process of law; nor deny to any person within its jurisdiction the equal protection of the laws**.

U.S. Constitution, Amendment 14

The Fourteenth Amendment was ratified in 1867. Over the next century and up to the present, the Amendment's requirements of due process and equal protection have been construed to have the effect of extending the Bill of Rights' protections to state actions, a process known as **incorporation**. Before that, the Bill of Rights protected citizens only against federal actions. The idea is that if states can't abridge due process – one of those usefully vague prohibitions – they can't, for example, abridge freedom of speech (First Amendment), unreasonably search (Fourth Amendment), compel self-incrimination (Fifth Amendment), deny criminal defendants access to attorneys (Sixth Amendment), etc. However, this incorporation has been a piecemeal process. Different elements of the Bill of Rights have been applied to states' action, one by one. Not all elements of the Bill of Rights have been incorporated;

for example the Third Amendment (forbidding quartering of soldiers in private homes in peacetime) has not, nor has the Seventh Amendment's right to a jury trial in civil (as contrasted with criminal) cases, although that Amendment's protection against courts' re-examining jury results has been. As of 2018, the most recent incorporation occurred in 2010, when *McDonald v. Chicago* extended the Second Amendment – that's the one protecting gun ownership – as construed in a 2008 decision, *District of Columbia v. Heller,* to state action.

The next case of interest was decided in 1936, the height of the Jim Crow era in the South. In Mississippi, three African-American men were arrested and charged with murdering a white man. To elicit confessions, they were beaten severely by police and civilians. Actually, "beaten severely" is an understatement. One defendant, before being arrested, was hung from a tree, twice, and when he was let down, he was tied to a tree and whipped. This action was led by a deputy sheriff. The suspect did not confess, yet. A day or two later he was arrested, by the same deputy and a colleague. During the drive to the jail, they stopped the car, took the suspect out, and whipped him, demanding his confession and threatening that the beating would continue until he agreed to confess to the crime in specific terms dictated by the deputy. At this point the man did so.

The other two suspects were arrested and brought to the jail. That night, the deputy, the jailer, another police officer, and some other men came to the jail, made the two men strip, and whipped them "until their backs were cut to pieces" and thereby forced to confess "in all particulars of detail so as to conform to the demands of their torturers" (*Brown v. Mississippi,* quoting *Brown v. State*).

The three men were found guilty in a one-day trial and sentenced to be hanged. When their appeal reached the Supreme Court, the Court unanimously overturned the convictions on Fourteenth Amendment due process grounds (not on Fifth Amendment grounds, because the Fifth Amendment had not yet been "incorporated").

"Due process" is, as was pointed out above, one of those wonderfully vague Constitutional word sequences. Literally, it means ... um

... legal process (e.g., trial) which is "due." Often courts apply "due process" to the facts of a case and state that the process involved violated something equally vague. In *Brown,* the Court wrote

8   The due process clause requires "that state action ... shall be consistent with the fundamental principles of liberty and justice which lie at the base of all our civil and political institutions." ... It would be difficult to conceive of methods more revolting to the sense of justice than those taken to procure the confessions of these petitioners, and the use of the confessions thus obtained as the basis for conviction and sentence was a clear denial of due process.

Brown v. Mississippi, 297 U.S. 278, 286 (1936)

So "due process" requires legal processes which are consistent with our "fundamental principles of liberty and justice," unlike the processes used against the *Brown* defendants. Actually, the vagueness doesn't give as much free rein to courts to simply apply their own values in cases as you might imagine; typically an opinion invoking a vague provision cites one or more (often several) previous cases to justify the interpretation and application in a given case. The *Brown* court did this, citing several previous Court decisions to support the due process basis for its decision.

In the 1950s and 1960s a series of Supreme Court decisions constrained what police were allowed to do to get confessions. In *Spano v. New York* (1959), police got a confession after an 8-hour overnight interrogation carried out without the presence of an attorney. The Court threw out the confession as involuntary on 14th Amendment due process grounds. Four justices in a **concurrence** (a separate opinion supporting the case's outcome) argued that the confession should have been excluded on Sixth Amendment right-to-counsel grounds ("In all criminal prosecutions...the accused shall enjoy the right to have assistance of counsel for his defense"). In 1961, police got a confession from a man by pretending to arrest the man's sick wife. The Court in *Rogers v. Richmond* threw the confession out on the grounds that that violated "fundamental decency" required by 14th Amendment due process. In *Townsend v. Sain* (1963), the Court overturned a conviction based on a confession induced by a "truth serum," because such a confession could not be the product of the person's free will. In 1963, *Gideon v. Wainwright* extended the Sixth Amendment's right to counsel to the states. This case has quite a story. Clarence Gideon had been arrested for a burglary of a pool hall in Panama City, Florida. He couldn't afford a lawyer and asked the trial court to appoint one for him, but the judge replied that under Florida law court-supplied attorneys were available only to defendants in death penalty cases. Gideon had to defend himself. By all accounts he did a good job for a layperson, but he was found guilty and was sentenced to five years in state prison. There, he became a pretty good jailhouse lawyer; despite having only an eighth grade education, he used the prison legal library and appealed to the Florida Supreme Court, where he lost, and then to the U.S. Supreme Court, where he won. After having to represent himself all along the way, at the Supreme Court level he was assigned the services of a prominent Washington lawyer, Abe Fortas, who was later a Supreme Court Justice. The Court unanimously held that the right to counsel in a criminal trial was fundamental and could not be denied to indigent defendants, writing:

[9]   [I]n our adversary system of criminal justice, any person haled into court, who is too poor to hire a lawyer, cannot be assured a fair trial unless counsel is provided for him. This seems to us to be an obvious truth... That government hires lawyers to prosecute and defendants who have the money hire lawyers to defend are the strongest indications of the widespread belief that lawyers in criminal courts are necessities, not luxuries.

Gideon v. Wainwright, 372 U.S. 335, 344 (1963)

In 1964, *Escobedo v. Illinois* followed the lead of the concurring justices in *Spano*, and held that the Sixth Amendment's right to counsel required the presence of a lawyer during police questioning, not just at trial, if the suspect sought it, and threw out a confession obtained after the suspect had repeatedly requested his attorney and the lawyer had actually come to the police station and had been turned away.

Also in 1964 another important case was decided, *Malloy v. Hogan*. A gambler named Malloy had spent three months in jail after being convicted, in a New Jersey state court, of illegal gambling. Out on probation, he was called to testify in a state investigation, but refused, on Fifth Amendment grounds. The Court finally extended the Fifth Amendment's protection against compelled self-incrimination to the states.

2.3 Conclusion

In this chapter you've encountered the law about detentions and made a start on the law about arrests and confessions, along with the linguistics needed to make sense of these matters – speech act theory and politeness theory. The point of this discussion is that linguistic analysis (here, speech act analysis) can be relevant to judicial decisionmaking, and that what courts actually do can be at odds with what linguistic analysis suggests. In the next chapter you'll grapple with the *Miranda* case and the "warning" it requires, seen from both legal history and linguistics.

Chapter 3

Miranda

3.0 Introduction

The facts of the *Miranda* case are simple. Ernesto Miranda was arrested in Phoenix, AZ, and charged with kidnapping and rape. The police questioned him for two hours, at the end of which he signed a form confessing to the rape. No lawyer was present nor was Miranda told that he had a right to remain silent or to have an attorney present. Miranda was convicted and sentenced to a long prison term. His appeal to the Arizona Supreme Court focused on the fact that the interrogation was conducted without the presence of an attorney. The court upheld Miranda's conviction on the grounds that he had not asked for one. Miranda's subsequent appeal to the U.S. Supreme Court led to one of the most significant Court decision in the area of criminal procedure in U.S. history, *Miranda v. Arizona*. The decision broadened the right against forced self-incrimination to cover all police questioning of suspects under arrest, going further than the 1950s and 1960s cases and holding that even without physical abuse or threats of it, the arrest context was inherently coercive enough to require explicit statements to arrestees of what their rights are, in order to protect those rights. Chief Justice Earl Warren's majority opinion can be seen as a predictable continuation of the trend summarized in Chapter 2 in cases from the 1950s and 1960s which provided progressively more protection of arrestees' Fifth, Sixth, and Fourteenth Amendment rights. But, as will be made clear below, it was a lot more than that; Warren's focus on the inherently disempowering situation of a police interrogation led to his identification of constitutionally required greater, and specific, protection of suspects' rights. However, given the treatment by the Supreme Court in several cases after *Miranda*, cutting back *Miranda* protections, the *Miranda* decision looks more like a pinnacle of arrestee protection.

Miranda has four holdings:

1   [I]f a person in custody is to be subjected to interrogation, he must first be informed in clear and unequivocal terms that he has the right to remain silent.

> *Miranda v. Arizona*, 384 U.S. 436, 467–468 (1966)

The warning of the right to remain silent must be accompanied by the explanation that anything said can and will be used against the individual in court...

> *Id.*, 469

[A]n individual held for interrogation must be clearly informed that he has the right to consult with a lawyer and to have the lawyer with him during interrogation...

> *Id.*, 471

In order fully to apprise a person interrogated of the extent of his rights under this system, then, it is necessary to warn him not only that he has the right to consult with an attorney, but also that, if he is indigent, a lawyer will be appointed to represent him.

> *Id.*, 473

These four holdings boil down to the more or less standard form of the warning:

2   You have the right to remain silent. Anything you say can and will be used against you in a court of law. You have the right to

speak to an attorney, and to have an attorney present during any questioning. If you cannot afford a lawyer, one will be provided for you at government expense.

The holdings, given in (1), permit variation in the wording, but police have to be careful not to change it too much, lest a court find them to have failed to meet the *Miranda* requirements.

Here are some tidbits from Warren's opinion, worth reading to get a feel for Warren's approach:

3   [T]he defendant was thrust into an unfamiliar atmosphere and run through menacing police interrogation procedures. The potentiality for compulsion is forcefully apparent... [S]uch an interrogation environment is created for no purpose other than to subjugate the individual to the will of his examiner. ...[T]his is not physical intimidation, but it is equally destructive of human dignity. ...[I]ncommunicado interrogation is at odds with one of our Nation's most cherished principles -- that the individual may not be compelled to incriminate himself.

Id., 457–458

4   An individual swept from familiar surroundings into police custody, surrounded by antagonistic forces, and subjected to the techniques of persuasion described above cannot be otherwise than under compulsion to speak.

Id., 461

The reference to "techniques of persuasion" pertains to specific police tactics Warren described. Warren went to some lengths to demonstrate the psychological pressure police could apply, quoting from police manuals. An example:

5   Where emotional appeals and tricks are employed to no avail, [the interrogator] must rely on an oppressive atmosphere of dogged persistence. He must interrogate steadily

and without relent, leaving the subject no prospect of sur-cease. He must dominate his subject and overwhelm him with his inexorable will to obtain the truth. He should interrogate for a spell of several hours, pausing only for the subject's necessities in acknowledgment of the need to avoid a charge of duress ... In a serious case, the interrogation may continue for days, with the required intervals for food and sleep, but with no respite from the atmosphere of domination. It is possible in this way to induce the subject to talk without resorting to duress or coercion.

> *Id.*, 451, quoting O'Hara, Fundamentals of Criminal Investigation (1956), 112

Yes, "without resorting to duress or coercion"!

3.1 Linguistic tricks police use

Some of the tactics Warren identifies are linguistic tricks. One is presupposing the suspect's guilt: "The interrogator should direct his comments toward the reasons why the subject committed the act, rather than court failure by asking the subject whether he did it" (*id.* 450). Because presuppositions are assumed as background facts, it takes communicative effort to challenge them. Also, because they're backgrounded, they can go unnoticed. Mistaken presuppositions – that is, presuppositions which an addressee actually does not already know to be true – are often simply accepted by addressees. This is known as **accommodation**. Example: Your tardy colleague explains: "Sorry I'm late. I had to take my sister to the hospital." You did not know, previously, that he had a sister. Because having a sister is uncontroversial, you have no trouble accepting the new-to-you proposition that he had one, never mind that it was inaccurately presented to you as a presupposition. Accommodation becomes progressively harder with more controversial presuppositions: "I had to take my car / unicycle / jet pack into the shop." Accommodation is facilitated by a power differential between conversational partners; if the presupposing speaker is the august CEO of the company you work for as a junior new employee, you may accept all manner of presuppositions whose content is actually new to you. In the arrest context, the power differential is extreme. Given this differential, along with cops' usual greater knowledge of the law governing arrest, post-arrest treatment of arrestees, and charging, and local prosecutors' charging practices, than most arrestees, it's easy to imagine successful manipulative use of presupposition by police.

A tactic related to presupposing guilt is to imply the possibility of legal excuses for the (possibly presupposed) criminal act: "You probably didn't go there intending to kill him. You probably brought your gun along because you knew he was dangerous. Anybody would have. You probably saw him go for his weapon and had to shoot him in self-defense."

Another linguistic trick is to try to induce suspects to confess by highlighting the Gricean expectation that speakers will provide enough information for current conversational needs (i.e., the maxim of Quantity), as in the bolded words below:

6   "Joe, you have a right to remain silent. That's your privilege, and I'm the last person in the world who'll try to take it away from you. If that's the way you want to leave this, O.K. But let me ask you this. **Suppose you were in my shoes, and I were in yours, and you called me in to ask me about this, and I told you, 'I don't want to answer any of your questions.' You'd think I had something to hide, and you'd probably be right in thinking that. That's exactly what I'll have to think about you, and so will everybody else.** So let's sit here and talk this whole thing over."

> *Id.*, 454, quoting Inbau and Reid, Criminal
> Interrogation and Confessions (1962), 111

3.2 Miranda *dissents*

The *Miranda* decision was 5–4. The dissenting justices argued that the pre-*Miranda* judicial stance regarding custodial confessions – looking at the "totality of the circumstances" surrounding a confession – worked fine, citing cases in which that approach had resulted in the exclusion from trial of forced confessions. To make a confession inadmissible, the total circumstances might include threats, physical deprivations such as lack of sleep or food, unreasonably long questioning sessions, restrictions on access to counsel, and suspects' incapacities. But the dissenters argued that in prior cases "no single default or fixed combinations of defaults guaranteed exclusion" (*id.*, Justice White, dissenting).

The most important of the dissenters' arguments (in their view and in public reaction) was a practical one, a prediction that requiring the communication of these four propositions to arrested suspects would gut law enforcement by significantly reducing the number of confessions. **At this point you should read Justice White's dissent.** (Do an internet search for the opinion – *Miranda v. Arizona,* 384 U.S. 436 (1966) – and scroll down to White's dissent.)

3.3 Reaction to the decision

Negative public reaction to the *Mirada* decision echoed the dissents' fears about its presumed crippling effect on police practice. With the warning that anything a suspect said would be used against them in court coupled with the statement that the suspect had the right to remain silent, why would anybody ever confess? A New York Times story about a conference for attorneys and law enforcement officers was headlined "*Miranda* Decision Said to End Effective Use of Confessions" (New York Times, August 21, 1966), and the story contained the following summary: "Panelists here agreed that the *Miranda* decision was a giant step toward the ultimate demise of the confession as a law enforcement tool." Editorial cartoons reflected this attitude, for example one by Charles Brooks (1966) published in the Birmingham News showing a person labeled "the criminal" driving a car labeled "Our criminal justice system" away from a spurned hitchhiker labeled "the victim." Public opinion polls showed widespread disapproval of the decision: a Harris poll taken a few months after the decision had 57% of respondents calling it "wrong" and only 30% calling it "right," and a Gallup poll taken shortly after *Miranda* had 63% of respondents feeling courts were too lenient, whereas Gallup had found – in a poll taken before *Miranda* – only 48% of respondents feeling that way (Peabody 2016).

In fact, these pessimistic views were wrong. While it's impossible to know for sure how many suspects confess – neither police nor other entities keep large-scale records that would show that – some extrapolations are possible from small data sets. As mentioned earlier, estimates are that 78%–96% of arrested suspects waive their *Miranda* rights and talk. Why? One suggestion is the "Stockholm syndrome," the emotional attachment hostages and prisoners sometimes feel toward individuals who have overwhelming power over them, their captors or guards. (The term derives from a 1973 bank robbery in Stockholm, Sweden, which developed into a six-day hostage situation in which some hostages became emotionally attached to the hostage-takers.) Another is ways police have adapted their interrogation techniques to take advantage of arrested suspects' weaknesses (lack of knowledge, low educational level, fear, hope, etc.). They follow the interrogation guidebooks referenced in Warren's opinion by interrogating in ways that convey to suspects that the suspects are powerless, and at the same time they build solidarity with suspects with friendly, first-name talk. They imply that the *Miranda* warning is just a bureaucratic necessity to be gotten out of the way before questioning. They try to persuade suspects to waive *Miranda* rights by implying that lenient treatment may ensue if suspects are cooperative, and, conversely, that harsher treatment – including harsher sentences – may follow from uncooperativeness.

All this may be more important in accounting for the prevalence of confessions than the linguistics of the *Miranda* warning. Nonetheless, the content of the warning is communicatively bizarre, and the bizarreness may contribute to getting suspects to confess.

3.4 Linguistic analysis of the **Miranda** *warning*

In its more or less standard form, the warning is organized into two pairs of pairs of sentences, with the sentences in each pair being mutually relevant (shown in (7)), and the two pairs also being mutually relevant (shown in (8)).

⁷ (1) You have a right to silence, [*which is needed because*] (2) anything you say can be used against you. (3) You have a right to an attorney, [*which implies*] (4) the state will pay for one if you can't afford it.

⁸ [*Because*] anything you say can be used against you (and so you have a right to silence) (1st pair), [*therefore*] an attorney to assist you is necessary (2nd pair).

Let's pretend again that you have been arrested. It doesn't matter whether you're guilty. The first thing you are told in the *Miranda* warning is that you have the right to remain silent. That doing so would be a good choice is reinforced by the next thing you're told: Anything you say will be used against you at your trial. So, being no dummy, you decide to keep your mouth shut. Right? Maybe so, after reading this chapter, but, as mentioned above, most suspects don't.

Grice's maxim of Quantity provides one explanation why so many suspects talk instead of sensibly remaining silent. That maxim reads "Make your contribution as informative as is required (for the current purposes of the exchange)." If you do talk, your "current purposes" are to explain your way out of the trouble you're in. The most direct way is to deny it, perhaps with supporting information like an alibi. You could also minimize your behavior; maybe what you did was self-defense, or a mistake, or – your fending off is getting weaker – you can't remember what happened.

Remaining silent not only feels like breaking a communicative rule; it also constitutes a **flouting** of the maxim, a violation of it so blatant that it can't be missed. The 5th Amendment's protection against compelled self-incrimination at trial permits witnesses to refuse to answer questions; doing so gives rise to the common understanding that "taking the 5th" means guilt. This can be demonstrated in a joke. The questioner is a prosecutor in a trial; the respondent is a witness.

⁹ Q. Did you ever spend the night with this man in New York?
A. I refuse to answer that question.
Q. Did you ever spend the night with this man in Chicago?
A. I refuse to answer that question.
Q. Did you ever spend the night with this man in Los Angeles?
[Several similar pairs of conversational turns]
Q. Did you ever spend the night with this man in Miami?
A. No.

The concept of flouting the maxim of Quantity has even found its way into a principle of law known as **adoptive admissions**. In its basics, this principle lets a jury decide whether a person's silence when the person heard statements "under such circumstances that the statements would have been denied if they were not true...was an admission of the truth of the statements." (Ninth Circuit Model Criminal Jury Instructions § 4.2 Silence In the Face of Accusation). Example: In your presence, your buddy Alan remarks to his friend Bill that you are pretty good at cracking safes. You don't say anything. Later, when you're on trial for safecracking, Bill testifies that you said nothing in the face of Alan's remark.

Adoptive admissions do not guarantee guilt, and the adoptive admissions rule above does not treat them as such; all it does is allow them in as evidence. Not responding to an utterance doesn't always constitute flouting of the maxim. One might not hear or understand it, or might not find it important. Or a person might not want to dignify an accusation with a response. Other contextual – pragmatically relevant – factors can operate too: fear (e.g., feeling intimidated by the statement's speaker or something else in the context), unwillingness to incriminate someone else, and all sorts of other specific context-specific factors. But courts don't always rule in accord with these common-sense observations. Adoptive admissions will get further attention in Chapter 4.

Perhaps, you might think, the next sentence in the warning – "Anything you say can and will be held against you" – might deter suspects from talking. But maybe not, since it obviously goes way too far: *anything* you say? A request to use the bathroom? For a drink of water? Answering a question about your age? Your address? This overinclusiveness might lead an arrested suspect to the mistaken conclusion that the warning is just a bureaucratic requirement not worth paying attention to. After all, lots of things happen in an arrest situation which the arrestee may not understand. More importantly, what about telling the police things which you think will get you off? How could they possibly be used against you? In fact they can, e.g., saying "I didn't kill him, Joe did" could inculpate a person just as a confession to pulling the trigger would. In jurisdictions where the crime of **felony murder** is on the books – almost all the states as well as federally – a person can be convicted of first degree murder without being the actual killer, if the person "participated" in a "dangerous" felony during which a murder occurred. The quotes point to obvious instances of vagueness, and there is some variation in how different jurisdictions deal with participation and danger. But in a jurisdiction with felony murder, pleading innocence by saying "I didn't do it, he did" would be a confession of guilt. How many arrestees know that? Consequently, it's not hard to imagine arrested subjects not taking this part of the warning as seriously as they should.

To make matters worse, two important facts are left out of the warning: First, evidence improperly obtained by violating rules – e.g., not giving the warning, or interrogating after giving it, without a suspect's waiver of rights – can be excluded from use at trial. Second, and much more immediately important for arrested suspects, there are no negative legal consequences that follow from not talking. This makes sense, given the right to silence: if you had a right to silence but that silence could be introduced as evidence against you, that would make your silence pointless. This exclusion from evidence is only fair, since it protects a defendant from the jury's natural inferring, under the maxim of Quantity, that silence means guilt. However, it took a Supreme Court decision to make this explicitly the law. In the 1976 case *Doyle v. Ohio*, defendants at trial provided an account which supported their innocence. The cross-examining prosecutor asked why they had not provided that account when they were arrested. The prosecutor's theory was that the defendants had come up with this exculpatory story later. This move worked; defendants were convicted. But on appeal to the Supreme Court, they won. The Court held that a person's silence after receiving the *Miranda* morning was "insolubly ambiguous"; it might be "nothing more than the arrestee's exercise of …*Miranda* rights."

Interestingly, the British analog of our *Miranda* warning takes the opposite position with respect to silence after arrest:

¹⁰ You do not have to say anything. But, it may harm your defence if you do not mention when questioned something which you later rely on in court. Anything you do say may be given in evidence.

www.gov.uk/arrested-your-rights

This warning provides a strong incentive to talk. So the British system uses the maxim of Quantity in its regular way, which in an arrest context means against suspects and defendants; the American system exempts suspects and defendants from the maxim of Quantity, but doesn't fully inform them of that.

In Chapter 5, language crimes will be discussed. One language crime is **perjury**, lying under oath about a material matter. A 1973 case, *Bronston v. United States,* will get attention. What happened in *Bronston* is relevant here. Bronston was found guilty for perjury for implicating something untrue. Asked whether he had bank accounts in Switzerland, he replied "The company had an account there, for about six months." This was true. But it was also true that Bronston had had a personal account with a bank in Switzerland. Bronston's answer deceptively implicated (by the maxim of Relevance, which says "Be relevant," as well as by our friend the maxim of Quantity) that he didn't, via the reasonable assumption that the company's having an account in Switzerland was a relevant and full answer to the question. On appeal to the Supreme Court, Bronston got his conviction reversed. The Court recognized the false implicature (though not by that name) but distinguished casual conversation from the adversarial talk between a witness and a cross-examining attorney, ruling that in the context of cross-examination, a good lawyer should recognize an evasive answer and follow up with further questions. It's not that the maxims of Relevance and Quantity are suspended in cross-examination; rather, attorneys are supposed to be able to recognize deceptive implicatures and know how to respond to them.

The Court's distinction in *Bronston* between casual conversation and courtroom testimony raises this question: Is a police interrogation more like an ordinary conversation or more like a conversation between a cross-examining attorney and a hostile witness? In its adversarial true nature – if the police arrest somebody, generally they're not disinterestedly seeking the truth; rather, they think they know the truth and are seeking proof of it – it's more like the latter. However, it is not clear that many arrested subjects know this, especially given the desire to exculpate oneself and the conversational tactics police use to minimize suspects' awareness of the adversarial reality they face. The *Miranda* warning might be expected to protect arrestees from the effects of these, but the warning, as we have seen, is communicatively strange.

3.5 *After* Miranda

What do the Fifth Amendment, and *Miranda*, guarantee? What does "be a witness against [one]self" – the wording in the Fifth Amendment – mean? The role of "being a witness against" necessarily involves communication; witnesses in court swear "to TELL the truth," etc., and when questioned they answer by making statements. With this in mind, consider the following scenario. You're an assistant district attorney prosecuting a man who has been arrested for drunk driving. Against his will, some of his blood was drawn and found to have a too-high alcohol concentration. In a pre-trial hearing, the drunkard's lawyer argued that the blood evidence should be disallowed as evidence on the grounds that (i) by being forced to have blood drawn, his client was compelled to be a witness against himself, in violation of the Fifth Amendment, (ii) drawing the blood violated the Fourth Amendment's protection against unreasonable searches and seizures, and (iii) it was a violation of 14th Amendment due process. Because – lucky you – linguistics had been your undergraduate major and you remember speech act theory from your semantics and pragmatics courses, you understand that what's involved in "being a witness" or "testifying" is the speech act of asserting. You figure out that the felicity conditions for the speech act of asserting are something like these:

11   Felicity conditions for asserting:

Semantic content :	Some proposition (i.e., something either true or false)
Preparatory condition:	Speaker believes that Addressee does not believe the proposition. (Note: not "disbelieves...," just "does not believe....")
Sincerity condition:	Speaker believes the proposition.
Essence:	(i) Counts as effort to add the proposition to the common ground;
	(ii) Counts as commitment to the truth of the proposition.

The Sincerity Condition is violated when speakers lie or otherwise intentionally mislead, resulting in an **abuse,** but not in a failure for the act of asserting to come off. These felicity conditions may not be exactly right, you say to yourself. For example, you're not entirely confident about the Preparatory Condition, because of "reminder" assertions, but on reflection you conclude that reminders fit fine, because at the time of the reminder, the Addressee appears to have forgotten, and thus temporarily not to know, the proposition. It occurs to you that an additional preparatory condition about evidence could be included: "Speaker has (or purports to have) evidence for the truth of the proposition." Second, you're not sure about the Sincerity Condition because hypotheticals ("OK, for the sake of argument, ghosts are real.") aren't necessarily believed by their speakers, but on reflection you decide that hypotheticals may not be Assertions. (They fail to meet the Preparatory Condition and Essence (ii).) All in all, the felicity conditions given in (11), maybe with the "evidence" bit added, seem reasonable. Note in particular the first "Essence": an assertion is an effort to do something; that is, it's an intentional act. Testifying – being a witness in court or analogous context – is intentional communication.

In fact, your memory of your semantics and pragmatics course in college is good enough for you to remember the analysis of the nature of communication put forward by Grice (1957): genuine communication occurs when a person says or does something intended to get an addressee to recognize not just the content of the intended message, but also the intent behind it – the intent to communicate. You even remember your very wonderful college instructor's example in lecture, which involved three scenarios. You're in a restaurant, impatient because you're not getting service. In scenario 1, you cough, inadvertently. A server notices and comes to take your order. Your cough is not communicative, because you didn't intend, by it, anything, and the server simply heard your cough and had his or her attention drawn to it just as if the noise had been any random noise coming from your direction. In scenario 2, you're getting really impatient, so you cough falsely, again inducing a server to notice and come to take your order. Although this time your behavior was intentional, it doesn't rise to the level of genuine communication, because all you intended was to alert the server to your presence by your (fictional) cold- or flu- generated cough, inducing the server, who thought it was a real cough, to respond, again, just as if it were any random noise coming from your direction. In scenario 3, you again cough falsely, this time exaggeratedly, so that no one would misunderstand it as a real cough. ("Mmm –ah-HEM!") This time the server recognizes your intention to communicate and comes over to take your order, this time maybe adding an apology lest your obvious irritation result in a small tip.

The scenario 3 level of intentionality characterizes what could be called prototypical human communication. It excludes unconscious responses to stimuli that result in a message being received, like a dog's happy tail wagging or a cat's angry tail lashing, which, if they are communicative at all, are so in a more limited way. In the same way your involuntary yell of pain or curse when you mistakenly hit your thumb with a hammer isn't prototypically communicative.

Finding an unlawful level of oxygen in blood drawn from a person is deriving a sort of "message," one that implies that the person who had that unlawful level of alcohol was probably drunk. But since the person did not intend to communicate that, it does not make sense to take the information gleaned from the blood to be testimonial, because it wasn't communicative. It's probably instead analogous to our inferring that Fido is happy from his wagging tail.

Because you not only have a great memory of your undergraduate linguistic work but are also an uncommonly articulate prosecutor, you find a way to communicate the essence of the linguistic analysis to the jury, without boring them silly with technical linguistics. Your linguistic analysis of communication overwhelms the weak defense claim that ascertaining the alcohol level in the defendant's blood was "testimonial." Awed by the power of your logic, the jury returns a verdict of "guilty" after five minutes of deliberation.

The facts as sketched above – blood drawn unwillingly after a drunk driving arrest – were the core facts in a 1966 Supreme Court case, *Schmerber v. California*, decided just a couple of months after *Miranda*. The defendant's argument was the same, that is, drawing the blood contravened the Fifth Amendment's proscription of compelled self-incrimination, the Fourth Amendment's protection against unreasonable searches, and the Fourteenth Amendment's requirement of due process. When the drunk driver's appeal reached the Supreme Court, the Supremes got it right, holding that the Fifth Amendment protected against compelled *testimony* against oneself and drawing blood which would then be analyzed was not testimony. In a similar case a year later, *U.S. v. Wade,* again the Court got it right, holding that being required to be part of a lineup and to say words the perpetrator of a robbery used did not constitute compelling "testimony." The uttering of the words in that way and context was not communicative; it was parroting.

In another 1967 case, *Gilbert v. California*, a suspect was required to give handwriting samples to see if they matched the handwriting on a note demanding money. The defense argued that that violated the defendant's Fifth Amendment right to be free from compelled self-incrimination. The Court held, correctly, that "[a] mere handwriting exemplar, in contrast to the content of what is written, like the voice or body itself, is an identifying physical characteristic outside [the Fifth Amendment's] protection."

The same sort of issue – what counts as compelled testimony – arose in a 1990 case. A man named Inocencio Muniz was arrested for drunk driving. At the police station, before being Mirandized, he was routinely processed, and was asked for factual information such as his name, height, weight, eye color, date of birth, and current age. Muniz stumbled answering a couple of these questions. The questioning was videotaped, so Muniz's slurred pronunciation was evident. The tape was allowed in as evidence. Muniz was convicted. When his appeal got to the Supreme Court, the Court – correctly – held that being unable to articulate well because of impaired oral muscle control was not testimonial. Given *Schmerber*, *Wade*, and *Gilbert*, this understanding by the Court should be no surprise, and what's more, should be seen as fitting within our linguistic understanding of communication, as conceived by both Grice and speech act theory (specifically the nature of the speech act of asserting). But there was one more part to Muniz's case. During the questioning before Muniz was Mirandized, the following interchange took place:

12   Officer: Do you know what the date was of your sixth birthday?
      Muniz: (Inaudible)
      Officer: When you turned six years old do you remember what the date was?
      Muniz: No, I don't.

Pennsylvania v. Muniz, 496 U.S. 582 (1990)

Was this testimonial? Was Muniz's admitted inability to remember or figure out the date of his sixth birthday testimonial in the Fifth

Amendment sense as expanded by *Miranda*? Muniz's "No, I don't" certainly incriminated him, since a non-intoxicated person could be expected to answer the question easily, and since this utterance was made before the *Miranda* warning was given, if it counts as testimonial, it should not have been admitted as evidence. Here is what the Court said:

13   [T]he inherently coercive environment created by the custodial interrogation precluded the option of remaining silent. Muniz was left with the choice of incriminating himself by admitting that he did not then know the date of his sixth birthday or answering untruthfully by reporting a date that he did not then believe to be accurate (an incorrect guess would be incriminating as well as untruthful). The content of his truthful answer supported an inference that his mental faculties were impaired, because his assertion (he did not know the date of his sixth birthday) was different from the assertion (he knew the date was [correct date]) that the trier of fact might reasonably have expected a lucid person to provide. Hence, the incriminating inference of impaired mental faculties stemmed, not just from the fact that Muniz slurred his response, but also from a testimonial aspect of that response. ... [B]ecause ... Muniz's response to the sixth birthday question was testimonial, the response should have been suppressed.

Id., 599

The Court's decision in this case was complicated, but this analysis the Court got right. Being "a witness against oneself" in the Fifth Amendment sense requires communication in the Gricean sense.

3.5.1 *Cutting back* Miranda

Since 1966, the year of *Miranda*, Supreme Court decisions have cut back the original *Miranda* protections. You'll see how different the orientation and approach in the majority opinions in these later cases are from Warren's in *Miranda*. The cutbacks have involved what counts as "interrogation," what suspects have to do to invoke their rights, and, relatedly, what counts as a suspect's waiving their *Miranda* rights. These will be discussed in turn. First, though, consider a case involving confusing wording in the version of the warning given. The key parts of the warning given are bolded:

14   Before we ask you any questions, you must understand your rights. You have the right to remain silent. Anything you say can be used against you in court. **You have a right to talk to a lawyer for advice before we ask you any questions, and to have him with you during questioning.** You have this right to the advice and presence of a lawyer even if you cannot afford to hire one. **We have no way of giving you a lawyer, but one will be appointed for you, if you wish, if and when you go to court.** If you wish to answer questions now without a lawyer present, you have the right to stop answering questions at any time. You also have the right to stop answering at any time until you've talked to a lawyer.

Duckworth v. Eagan, 492 U.S. 195, 198 (1989)

The *Miranda* decision did not specify what words or phrases police have to use, and there is some variation in wording in different jurisdictions. In this case, the two bolded parts seem contradictory. A person could easily take the two boldfaced sentences above as having the contradictory meaning "You can have a lawyer before and during questioning, but we can't provide one for you unless or until you go to court." In fact, isn't that all they could mean? Actually, no, as you will see from the Supreme Court's decision in a moment.

The defendant in the case, Gary Eagan, was convicted of attempted murder. (He had stabbed someone.) On appeal, the Seventh Circuit reversed, finding that the statement that counsel would be appointed "if and when you go to court" did not give an arrestee clear information that he had a right to a lawyer before questioning and wrongly connected a person's right to counsel before questioning to a future event, making the warning given unconstitutional. The Supreme Court reversed the reversal, in a 5–4 decision authored by Chief Justice Rehnquist. Notice how different the approach is from that of Warren's in *Miranda*:

[15] We think the initial warnings given to respondent touched all of the bases required by *Miranda*. First, this instruction accurately described the procedure for the appointment of counsel in Indiana. Under Indiana law, counsel is appointed at the defendant's initial appearance in court…[I]t must be relatively commonplace for a suspect, after receiving *Miranda* warnings, to ask when he will obtain counsel. The "if and when you go to court" advice simply anticipates that question. Second, *Miranda* does not require that attorneys be producible on call, but only that the suspect be informed, as here, that he has the right to an attorney before and during questioning, and that an attorney would be appointed for him if he could not afford one. The Court in *Miranda* emphasized that it was not suggesting that "each police station must have a station house lawyer' present at all times to advise prisoners." If the police cannot provide appointed counsel, *Miranda* requires only that the police not question a suspect unless he waives his right to counsel.

Duckworth v. Eagan, 492 U.S. 195, 203 (1989)

So a suspect has the right to attorney during interrogation, but that doesn't mean he gets one; it just means that if he doesn't get one he can't be interrogated.

The dissent (Marshall, joined by Brennan, Blackmun, and Stevens) disagreed with this approach:

[16] Under *Miranda*, a police warning must "clearly infor[m]" a suspect taken into custody "that, if he cannot afford an attorney, one will be appointed for him prior to any questioning, if he so desires." A warning qualified by an "if and when you go to court" caveat does nothing of the kind; instead, it leads the

suspect to believe that a lawyer will not be provided until some indeterminate time in the future...

...

Upon hearing the warnings given in this case, a suspect would likely conclude that no lawyer would be provided until trial. ... Furthermore, the negative implication of the caveat is that, if the suspect is never taken to court, he "is not entitled to an attorney at all."

Duckworth v. Eagan, 492 U.S. 195 (1989),
Marshall, J., dissenting

3.5.1.1   What counts as interrogation?

Consider the following scenario. A man is arrested for an abduction which occurred 160 miles away from where he is arrested. He has to be driven by the police to the city where the abduction occurred. He is told by his lawyer not to say anything to the police on the drive there. The two police detectives taking him there agree not to question him during the drive. The officers know that the man is very religious. One of them says the following, addressing the subject as "Reverend":

17   I want to give you something to think about while we're traveling down the road... Number one, I want you to observe the weather conditions, it's raining, it's sleeting, it's freezing, driving is very treacherous, visibility is poor, it's going to be dark early this evening. They are predicting several inches of snow for tonight, and I feel that you yourself are the only person that knows where this little girl's body is, that you yourself have only been there once, and if you get snow on top of it you yourself may be unable to find it. And, since we will be going right past the area on the way into Des Moines, I felt that we could stop and locate the body, that the parents of this little girl should be entitled to a Christian burial for the little girl who was snatched away from them on Christmas [E]ve and

murdered. And I feel we should stop and locate it on the way in, rather than waiting until morning and trying to come back out after a snow storm, and possibly not being able to find it at all.

Brewer v. Williams, 430 U.S. 387, 392–393 (1977)

In speech act terms, what is this? A speech act of questioning? A speech act of requesting, specifically a request to the prisoner to take the officers to the victim's body?

First, then, is the discourse a speech act of questioning? Setting aside "exam questions," to which the speaker knows the answer and is trying to find out whether the addressee does, and rhetorical questions, which are really assertions in disguise, the point of ("information") questions is to find out either whether some proposition is true (e.g., Yes / No questions) or to complete some proposition which has a gap (so-called "open" questions, typically exemplified by *wh*-questions). So the felicity conditions for questioning are something like these:

18 Felicity conditions for questioning:

Semantic content:	Some proposition
Preparatory conditions:	Speaker (i) does not know the complete proposition or (ii) does not know whether the complete proposition is true.
	Speaker wants to know (i) the complete proposition or (ii) whether it is true.
	Speaker believes that Addressee knows (i) the complete proposition or (ii) whether it is true.
Essence:	Counts as effort to get answer from Addressee.

The speech act of questioning has three direct, conventional forms, inversion of the subject and auxiliary verb without a *wh*-word (e.g., *Did you kill her?*), such inversion with one (e.g., *Where did you bury the body?*), and performative form (*I (hereby) ask you...*) Other utterances that function as questions are indirect speech acts, such the following:

> *Can you / could you / I wonder if you could tell me...*
> *Do you know...,*
> *I'd like to know...*

The policeman's speech in ex. (17) has none of these, nor any direct question forms. What it has – in order of occurrence – are:

- requests in the form of statements ("I want to give you something to think about," "I want you to observe the weather conditions"),
- assertions ("it's going to be dark early this evening," "you yourself are the only person who knows where this little girl's body is," "you yourself have only been there once," If you get snow on top of it you yourself may be unable to find it"),
- a suggestion in the form of a statement ("I felt that we could stop and locate the body"),
- a moral assertion ("the parents of this little girl should be entitled to a Christian burial..."), and
- another suggestion in the form of a statement ("I feel we should stop and locate it on the way in").

Most of these speech acts are indirect, for example the request encoded in the first sentence: "I want to give you something to think about..." The request to think about something is encoded in what is literally a statement about the speaker's feelings: "I want..." The assertions are the only direct speech acts: "it's going to be dark early this evening," etc. Now, what about the whole speech?

Looking at the felicity conditions for questioning in ex. (18), it fits. The semantic content is something like *The body is at such-and-such location*, or perhaps simply *I killed her*. All three of the

Preparatory Conditions are met: The speaker doesn't know the answer, wants to know it, and believes the Addressee does know it. And the Essence is satisfied as well. The only reason for the police officer to go on as he did was to elicit the answer. The speech was directed to the suspect, the referent of all the occurrences of *you* in the speech. And the speech worked; it turns out that the suspect ended up leading the police to the victim's shoes, in another place to her blanket, and finally to her body.

Under a "Request" analysis, there's a fit too. The felicity conditions for requesting were given in Chapter 2. Here they are again:

19   Felicity conditions for requests

Semantic content:	Future act by Addressee
Preparatory conditions:	Speaker believes Addressee can carry out the future act
	It's not obvious that Addressee would carry out the act without being requested
Essence:	Counts as non-enforceable attempt to get Addressee to carry out the act

The semantic content is either the suspect's leading the officers to the victim's body or confessing to the crime. As for the Preparatory Conditions, clearly the detective believes the suspect can do these things and it's not obvious he will without being requested. And the Essence works too; there can be no doubt that the officer is by his words trying to get the suspect to confess by word or deed.

The Supreme Court saw it that way too, overturning the conviction because the interrogation violated *Miranda*.

A superficially similar case three years later had a different outcome. A man named Thomas Innis was arrested for robbing a cab driver with a sawed-off shotgun. He was given the *Miranda* warning. The shotgun was missing. He was driven to the police station in a police car with three officers, who were instructed not to question him. On the way, two of the officers talked between themselves about the missing shotgun. One of the officers said there were "a lot of handicapped children running around in this area" because a school for such children was nearby, and "God forbid one of them might find a weapon with shells and they might hurt themselves." Innis interrupted and told the officers he would show them where the shotgun was. And he did just that, saying he "wanted to get the gun out of the way because of the kids in the area in the school." He was convicted at trial. Relying in part on *Brewer v. Willliams*, the Rhode Island supreme court set aside the conviction and held that the officers had "interrogated" Innis without a valid waiver of his *Miranda* rights.

Did the officers "interrogate" Innis? The Supreme Court said No. Here is the holding and explanation for it from the majority opinion:

[20] [T]he term "interrogation" under *Miranda* refers not only to express questioning, but also to any words or actions on the part of the police ... that the police should know are reasonably likely to elicit an incriminating response from the suspect.

...

[But] [i]t cannot be said...that Patrolmen Gleckman and McKenna should have known that their conversation was reasonably likely to elicit an incriminating response from the respondent. There is nothing in the record to suggest that the officers were aware that the respondent was peculiarly susceptible to an appeal to his conscience ... Nor is there anything in the record to suggest that the police knew that the respondent was unusually disoriented or upset ... [T]he entire conversation appears to have consisted of no more than a few offhand remarks...

Rhode Island v. Innis, 446 U.S. 291, 292 (1980)

Unlike in *Brewer v. Williams*, here the suspect was not directly addressed, nor did the police knowingly take advantage of any psychological weaknesses he might have had. According to the Court, the police just had a conversation among themselves. That seems to have made all the difference, to the Court majority. Interestingly, the majority zeroed in on the policemen's expectations, writing "it cannot be said … that [they] should have known that their conversation was reasonably likely to elicit an incriminating response…" Another approach might have been to consider the policemen's intent, which was presumably to have the exact perlocutionary effect their words had on Innis. Under the felicity conditions for questions and requests ((18) and (19) above), the policemen's conversation would fit, except, possibly, for the identity of the Addressee. Superficially the Addressee was just the other officer, not the suspect Innis. But really? **Now read Justice Marshall's (scathing) dissent**.

3.5.1.2   *What do you have to do to invoke your rights?*

The *Miranda* decision guarantees two rights to arrestees, the right to silence and the right to an attorney during questioning. These two rights are related in that once an arrestee says they want an attorney, questioning has to stop. As long as an arrestee says nothing, they don't have to do anything to use the right to silence, but saying nothing will not necessarily halt questioning. Requesting an attorney will, at least if it's done right. So how should you, if (gods forbid) you're arrested, request an attorney? This might seem like a strange question; everybody knows how to make requests. We do it all the time:

> "Can you pass me the salt?"
> "I wonder if you could possibly open the window."
> "I'd like the veggie omelet."
> "Why don't you stand over there?"
> "Let me in, would you?"

And, as we saw in the previous chapter, "Do you mind if I look in the trunk?" All of these, if they are requests, as they are in most contexts, are indirect. We hardly ever use the imperative form for a request; "Give me a pencil" sounds more like an order than a request, and if the context favors requests rather than commands, it sounds rude. We use indirect speech acts to make requests polite, preserving the face of addressees. Given the dramatic power difference between police officers and arrestees, deference is in order. A request for an attorney might be expected to occur in a form like "I guess maybe I should talk to an attorney." Believe it or not, that might not work. The Court has taken a restrictive view of what kinds of utterances count as requests for an attorney. The law on this was created by the holding in *Davis v. U.S.* (1994):

21 [I]f a suspect makes a reference to an attorney that is ambiguous or equivocal in that a reasonable officer in light of the circumstances would have understood only that the suspect might be invoking a right to counsel, our precedents do not require the cessation of questioning.

[T]he suspect must unambiguously request counsel.

Davis v. U.S., 512 U.S. 452, 459 (1994)

This is not so bad, you might think, with "a reasonable officer's" reaction to words that only "might" be a request for counsel. In fact many of the utterances which defense lawyers have claimed at trial to have been requests for attorneys have been found by courts to be ambiguous. Here is a list, from Solan & Tiersma (2005):

22 Utterances held not to be requests for an attorney

...feel like I might want to talk to an attorney
I think I would like to talk to a lawyer.
Wait a minute. Maybe I ought to have an attorney. You guys are trying to pin a murder rap on me, give me 20 or 40 years.
Maybe I need a lawyer.
I think I might need a lawyer.
If I'm going to be charged with murder maybe I should talk to an attorney.
Didn't you say I had the right to an attorney?

If you are ever (gods forbid) arrested, and you want an attorney (as you should), please say the following or something like these: "I hereby request an attorney" or "Get me an attorney."

Invoking one's right to a lawyer is closely related to waiving one's *Miranda* rights, to which we now turn.

3.5.1.3 How does a person waive their rights? What is the meaning of silence and of talking?

If a person waives (gives up) a right, they give up their entitlement to do something, or permit something to be done which otherwise they might not allow. This second kind of waiving sounds a lot like consenting, a speech act discussed in Chapter 2. A distinctive feature of consenting, you might remember, is the requirement that the consent be sincere. But waiving a right has no sincerity condition. Waiving is a formal legal act. Possibly the only situations in which you have waived a right are in the context of non-negotiable contracts. Some contracts require waiving the right to sue; instead, if there's a dispute, arbitration is required. To waive the right to sue, you don't have to sincerely want to; in fact you may prefer not to but you have no choice, if you want to form the contract.

Here are the felicity conditions for waiving:

23   Felicity conditions for the speech act of waiving:

Semantic content:	A legal right
Preparatory conditions:	(i) The speaker has the legal right. (ii) The speaker has the right to relinquish it. (iii) The speaker is not obliged to relinquish it.
Essence:	Counts as the speaker's giving up the legal right.

Preparatory condition (iii) doesn't contradict waiving a right in order to form a contract; waiving in such a context is still optional. All choosing not to waive means is that you won't agree to the contract.

As with almost all speech acts, waiving need not be explicit. As you might expect, the tricky part about waiving in the context of an arrest is how to establish that a person has waived a right, when the person has not explicitly said he or she is doing so. *Miranda* requires the prosecution to meet a "heavy burden":

24   If the interrogation continues without the presence of an attorney and a statement is taken, a heavy burden rests on the government to demonstrate that the defendant knowingly and intelligently waived his privilege against self-incrimination and his right to retained or appointed counsel.

> *Miranda v. Arizona, op. cit.*

Remember *Brewer v. Williams*, the case involving the suspect's long ride with the police during which a policeman addressed the suspect with the "Christian burial" speech ((17) above)? Did Robert Williams waive his right to silence?

The state courts said Yes. They said that the suspect did not assert his right to counsel, nor did he express a desire not to give information to the police without an attorney. Actually, Williams did say several times during the trip that he would talk after consulting with his lawyer at the end of the trip, which implicates, by Quantity, that he would not talk during the trip.

The Supreme Court saw things exactly this way:

25   [Williams's] statements while in the car that he would tell the whole story after seeing [his lawyer] in Des Moines were the clearest expressions by Williams himself that he desired the presence of an attorney before any interrogation took place.

> *Brewer v. Williams, op. cit.*

The dissent argued that since Williams had been told that he need not talk to police during the drive, and during the drive he told the police that he would tell them the whole story when they got to their destination and he talked with his attorney, he knew he was entitled to wait until counsel was present. His talking anyway showed a waiver.

If you are skeptical about the dissent's argument, would it would be more persuasive with a different suspect? Let's change the story. Instead of a former mental patient, let's make the suspect a 3rd year law student, or a law professor, or even a professor of linguistics with a law degree. Now, if that person talks, is this a real waiver?

Consider now a case from 1979. A man named Willie Butler was involved in an armed robbery of a gas station during which the gas station attendant was shot and wounded. When he was arrested he was Mirandized, but refused to sign a form saying he understood and was waiving his *Miranda* rights: "I will talk to you but I am not signing any form." And talk he did, telling officers he and his friend Elmer Lee had been drinking and decided to rob the gas station, but that he had not actually participated in the robbery and Lee was the one who shot the attendant. At trial he was convicted of kidnapping, armed robbery, and felonious assault. On appeal, the North Carolina Supreme Court overturned the conviction on the grounds that Butler had not waived his right to counsel either in writing or orally. Here's the relevant part of *Miranda* that supported this approach:

[26] An individual need not make a pre-interrogation request for a lawyer. While such request affirmatively secures his right to have one, his failure to ask for a lawyer does not constitute a waiver. No effective waiver of the right to counsel during interrogation can be recognized unless specifically made after the warnings we here delineate have been given.

Miranda v. Arizona, op. cit.

However, the 1979 (U.S.) Supreme Court construal of the 1966 *Miranda* language above was that "specifically made" does not require explicit speech:

[27] An express written or oral statement of waiver of the right to remain silent or of the right to counsel … is not

> inevitably ... necessary ... [I]n at least some cases, waiver can be clearly inferred from the actions and words of the person interrogated.
>
> *North Carolina v. Butler*, 441 U.S. 369 (1979)

How does this compare with *Brewer v. Williams* and *Innis*?

Next consider a 2010 case, *Berghuis v. Thompkins*. Thompkins was arrested for homicide and was Mirandized. During a three-hour interrogation he was almost entirely silent. He never requested an attorney or said he wasn't going to talk; he just kept his mouth shut. Finally, the police changed their tactics and asked him whether he believed in God, whether he prayed to God, and whether he prayed to God to forgive him for shooting the victim. (Notice the presuppositions!) He answered "yes" to each of these. Oops. He was found guilty. On appeal, his conviction was reversed. The appellate court reasoned that Thompkins's "persistent silence for nearly three hours in response to questioning and repeated invitations to tell his side of the story offered a clear and unequivocal message to the officers: Thompkins did not wish to waive his rights" (appellate court opinion, quoted in the majority opinion when the case got to the Supreme Court). The state appealed to the Supreme Court, and ... (drum roll)... won! The Sixth Circuit's decision was overturned, 5–4. The majority cited the *Davis* decision (see above), the one that held that a suspect has to invoke the right to counsel unambiguously, and extended that rule to the right to silence:

28 [T]here is no principled reason to adopt different standards for determining when an accused has invoked the *Miranda* right to remain silent and the *Miranda* right to counsel...

> *Berghuis v. Thompkins*, 560 U.S. 370 (2010)

According to the Court, (i) it makes sense to use the same "no ambiguity" rule for invoking not only the right to counsel, but also the right to silence; (ii) the "no ambiguity" rule creates a usefully objective standard police can use which (iii) will make for fewer "lost" confessions, thereby better serving the public policy of convicting criminals.

The four dissenters' (Justices Sotomayor, Stevens, Ginsburg, and Breyer) view was different, and included a communicative rationale:

29 [S]tatements or actions – in particular, when a suspect sits silent throughout prolonged interrogation,… – cannot reasonably be understood other than as an invocation of the right to remain silent…

Id.

The dissent also pointed to the contradiction between being told that one has the right to silence and a rule that one has to speak in order to protect oneself against being found to have waived the right:

30 The Court … concludes that a suspect who wishes to guard his right to remain silent against such a finding of "waiver" must, counterintuitively, speak…

Id.

Now consider this one. A guy answers questions from police about a killing. He is not under arrest (and, naturally, has not been Mirandized). But when the cops ask him if ballistics testing would reveal that shell casings recovered from the location of the killing would match his shotgun, he is silent. Remember "adoptive admissions?" A person's silence when a contextual utterance implicating the person's guilt is made can be allowed in at trial as evidence of the person's guilt. That's what happened in *Salinas v. Texas,* a 2013 case. At trial, despite the defense's objection, the prosecution was allowed to argue that Salinas's silence to the question about ballistic testing of shell casings was evidence of his guilt. Salinas was convicted. On appeal, the Texas Court of Appeals upheld his conviction on the grounds that his pre-arrest silence was not in a "compulsion" context in the Fifth Amendment sense. And when his appeal got to the Supremes, they echoed this argument, distinguishing a non-custodial questioning from the "uniquely coercive nature of custodial interrogation," and upheld the conviction, on the grounds that Salinas had not expressly invoked his Fifth Amendment right. **You should now read *Salinas v. Texas*.**

The holdings in the cases discussed above involving waiving *Miranda* rights and the significance for that of both silence and speaking are summarized chronologically below:

31   Waiving, keeping silent, and speaking: a time line

Brewer v. Williams (1977): Talking doesn't waive if the suspect was interrogated in violation of *Miranda*.
N.C. v. Butler (1979): Non-compelled talking is a waiver.
R.I. v. Innis (1980): Talking waives if there was no interrogation.
U.S. v. Davis (1994): Invocation of the right to counsel must be unambiguous.
Berghuis v. Thompkins (2010): Finally speaking, after a long silence, counts as a waiver.
Salinas v. Texas (2013): Non-custodial silence is admissible as an adoptive admission; silence does not constitute invoking a right.

3.5.1.4 What happens with cognitively limited suspects: mentally ill people and children?

Consider the story of Francis Connelly. Connelly walked up to a Denver policeman and told him he had committed a murder. It turned out that Connelly was schizophrenic and believed the voice of God had commanded him – literally; he heard voices - to confess. Was this a valid waiver? Under the felicity conditions given above in ex. (23), Yes; waiving is simply a legal act of relinquishing a right without compulsion. But should there be a requirement of basic rationality, of being at least more or less in touch with reality? Should the felicity conditions of all speech acts include basic sanity, that is, freedom from hallucinations or other impossible false beliefs? In this chapter we have discussed (or at least mentioned) the speech acts of asserting, consenting, ordering, promising, questioning, requesting, and waiving. Certainly no such basic sanity is required to assert, order, promise, question, or request. It doesn't matter how crazy you are, "Please give me some money" is a request. How about consenting? Consenting requires sincerity, unlike the other acts, but sincerity obviously is not equivalent to sanity. In the previous chapter, the nature of consenting was discussed in connection with *Schneckloth v. Bustamonte*, the case about consenting to a police search. Both the majority and the dissenters saw a role for the mental state of the person consenting, both zeroing in on the same factor, voluntariness, but neither considered whether a person's craziness could prevent legitimate consent.

The majority and the dissent in *Colorado v. Connelly* are instructive. The majority's view, and the holding of the case, was that (in)sanity was irrelevant; all that mattered for a valid waiver, or a confession, was the absence of police coercion:

³² *Miranda* protects defendants against government coercion leading them to surrender rights protected by the Fifth Amendment; it goes no further than that.

...

[C]oercive police activity is a necessary predicate to the finding that a confession is not "voluntary"...

Colorado v. Connelly, 479 U.S. 157 (1986)

Does this mean that by 1986 we had come full circle back to the pre-*Miranda* scene, when all that mattered was whether clear coercion was applied to arrestees in custody? Maybe not, because in *Connelly* the facts involved a non-custodial confession; the holding in *Connelly* is not inconsistent with the *Miranda* view that custody after arrest is inherently coercive. But the attitude of the Court, the "feel" of the majority opinion, is quite different. **You should now read Justice Steven's concurrence and Justice Brennan's dissent (joined by Justice Marshall).**

How about kids? Should, in certain contexts, the age of a suspect affect whether someone is "in custody," triggering the requirement that the *Miranda* warning be given? It might seem strange to frame the issue that way; isn't being in custody pretty obvious? Not necessarily. Custody was defined in *Miranda* straightforwardly: having one's freedom constrained in an overtly and substantial way. This formulation was sharpened by later cases to include the objective standard of whether a reasonable person in the suspect's position would have felt free to leave. With that in mind, consider this: A 13-year old seventh grader, "J.D.B.," was called out of his social studies class into a school conference room, and questioned, by two school administrators and two police officers, about some break-ins. He was not told he was under arrest (he wasn't) and he was not Mirandized. His grandmother, with whom he lived, was not contacted. In interrogating him, the police used the same sort of tactics discussed earlier. The assistant principal urged the boy to "do the right thing" and told him "the truth always comes out in the end." What else happened in the principal's office was summarized by Justice Sotomayor in her majority opinion in *J.D.B. v. North Carolina*, 564 U.S. 261 (2011), **which you should now read.**

3.5.1.5 Summarizing the post-Miranda history

The following timeline of *Miranda* cases sums up the history of how the *Miranda* protections have been cut back over the years since at least 1979:

1966	*Miranda*	
1976	Doyle v. Ohio:	Post-*Miranda*-warning silence cannot be used against one. An extension of *Miranda*.
1977	Brewer v. Williams:	"Interrogation" construed broadly. Waiver not found under facts of the case ("Christian burial" speech directed to suspect). An extension.
1979	North Carolina v. Butler:	Waiver of *Miranda* rights can be found from a course of conduct. *Miranda* had held that a waiver of the right to counsel required the suspect to "specifically" waive. A cutting back.

1980	R.I. v. Innis:	Between-officer conversation, within hearing of suspect, with intent to elicit inculpating information, about danger of weapon to public not within the definition of "interrogation" A cutting back.
1986	Colorado v Connelly:	"Voluntariness" limited to "freedom from state coercion"; a mentally ill confession admissible. A cutting back.
1989	Duckworth v. Eagan:	Permitted: probably misleading and almost certainly confusing wording of the part of the warning about access to attorney. A cutting back.
1994	Davis v. U.S.:	To invoke the right to counsel, unambiguous request necessary. A cutting back.
2010	Berghuis v. Thompkins:	To invoke the right to silence, suspect must say so. Relying on *Davis*, invocation must be unambiguous. Waiving: Relying on *North Carolina v. Butler*, a waiver need not be express. An uncoerced statement establishes an implied waiver. A cutting back.

This chronology leaves out an important case. In 2000, the Supreme Court decided *Dickerson v. U.S.* The facts were simple. Dickerson gave an inculpating statement to FBI agents after being arrested but before being given the *Miranda* warning. The statement was inadmissible at trial, right? Nope. It came in, and Dickerson was convicted of bank robbery. Now things get a little complicated. Dickerson's statement was allowed in as evidence because of a law Congress had passed in 1968, in response to the outcry from "law and order" opinion makers, including presidential candidate Richard Nixon, about the predicted harm to public safety and the compromises to justice that were expected to ensue from *Miranda*. The statute, called the "Omnibus crime control and safe streets act," 42 U.S.C. § 3501, repealed the strict warning requirements of *Miranda* – or purported to. In place of the strong *Miranda* requirements, it reinstated voluntariness: a confession would be admissible in federal prosecutions "if it is voluntarily given," even if the *Miranda* warning was not given. Despite being passed by Congress and signed into law by President Lyndon Johnson, the statute was never relied on and never tested for its constitutionality, about which there were doubts. Congress can't pass unconstitutional laws (or if it does they will presumably be struck down when challenged), and the assumption was that *Miranda* was "constitutionally based," in other words it manifested a Constitutional requirement. So, a law that overturned *Miranda* was on the books, but ignored – that is, until Dickerson's legal troubles made their way through the appeals process. What happened was that Dickerson's lawyer moved to have Dickerson's statement thrown out because it had been obtained in violation of *Miranda*, and won. The prosecution appealed to the Fourth Circuit, where the trial court's decision was overturned, on the basis of the 1968 statute, reviving it from its moribund status. The Supreme Court took Dickerson's appeal and affirmed the general understanding of the statute, namely, that it was unconstitutional:

[33]   In *Miranda v. Arizona*, 384 U.S. 436 (1966), we held that certain warnings must be given before a suspect's statement made during custodial interrogation could be admitted in evidence. In the wake of that decision, Congress enacted 18 U.S.C. § 3501 which in essence laid down a rule that the admissibility of such statements should turn only on whether or not they were voluntarily made. We hold that *Miranda*, being a constitutional decision of this Court, may not be in effect overruled by an Act of Congress, and we decline to overrule *Miranda* ourselves. We therefore hold that *Miranda* and its progeny in this Court govern the admissibility of statements made during custodial interrogation in both state and federal courts.

Dickerson v. U.S., 530 U.S. 428 (2000)

This outcome was a surprise. *Miranda* had been so weakened by 2000 that the expectation was that the Court would deal it a final death blow and just overturn it. The surprise at the result was underscored by the fact that the author of the majority opinion was Chief Justice William Rehnquist, a conservative figure for whom "law and order" was a paramount concern. One stated reason for the decision was interesting: *Miranda* "has become embedded in routine police practice to the point where the warnings have become part of our national culture." *Id.*

And that's the way it stands today: the *Miranda* warning is constitutionally required, but a waiver of both the right to counsel during questioning and the right to silence can be inferred from an arrestee's talking (*Butler, Berghuis*); what counts as interrogation is understood narrowly (*Innis*); insanity is not a bar to a confession being used against a defendant (*Connelly*); and non-ambiguity is required for both a request for counsel and a claim of the right to silence (*Davis, Berghuis*).

3.6 Summary and conclusion

In this chapter and the previous one, we have explored the communications at the center of police detentions and arrests, and the parts of linguistic theory that contribute to understanding them, namely speech act theory and Gricean implicature. Both detentions and arrests are subject to Constitutional restrictions which most detainees and arrestees don't know, a fact which police use in their communications with individuals subject to their control. In detentions, police often clothe requests to search with politeness, preserving detainees' face, thereby sometimes getting detainees' consent to searches otherwise impermissible (and against detainees' interests). When courts address such apparent consent, under *Schneckloth v. Bustamonte*, they characterize the nature of consent as not including a person's knowledge that they have the right to refuse consent. In the arrest context, a series of Supreme Court cases culminating in *Miranda v. Arizona* prevent police from abusing suspects physically and psychologically to get them to provide inculpatory evidence, but they can use communicative tactics aimed to produce the same result. The potential effect of these tactics is, ironically, accelerated by the *Miranda* warning, which is communicatively confusing. The warning tells people that they can remain silent, a surprising fact in the context of an accusation of having committed a crime, and that anything they do say may be used against them at trial, an overbroad statement which may therefore be discounted. The communicative oddness of the warning may contribute to the frequency of suspects' disregarding the warning and talking.

The decades since *Miranda* have seen considerable cutbacks by the Supreme Court of the protections created by the *Miranda* decision. What counts as "interrogation" was circumscribed in *Rhode Island v. Innis* to exclude talk between officers designed to elicit inculpating verbal responses from suspects, an interpretation that ignores the role of intention behind speech. What suspects have to do to invoke their Miranda rights was limited in *Davis v. U.S.* to unambiguous requests. What counts as waiving *Miranda* rights was defined in *North Carolina v. Butler* and *Berghuis v. Thompkins* to include "actions and words" such as finally speaking after a long period of silence, during questioning, an interpretation arguably at odds with the *Miranda* opinion's holding that a waiver must be explicit. *Salinas v. Texas* allowed a suspect's silence in the context of a police question to be admissible at trial, when the conversation between police and suspect was pre-arrest. This comports with Gricean Quantity but contradicts the protections *Miranda* provides to suspects; the Court could make this move because a non-arrest context is devoid of *Miranda* protection.

Throughout this discussion, wherever possible speech act theory and the Gricean understanding of rational communication have provided a lens to understand what goes on communicatively in detention and arrest contexts. We will use these parts of linguistic theory, as well as other areas of linguistics, in later chapters as well.

Additional worthwhile readings

There is a large body of literature about *Miranda*. Listing a few items here is not intended to implicate anything negative about others. Three useful books are Wrightsman & Pitman 2010, Leo 2008, and Leo & Thomas 1998. Two journal articles of linguistic interest are Shuy 1997 and Ainsworth 2011.

Chapter 4

Understanding recorded talk

4.0 Introduction

"Who said it?" Suppose a bomb threat has been called in. A suspect is arrested, a worker known to bear a grudge against his employer. He denies making the call, but his superiors, and the police, think the caller's voice sounds like his. Can voices be matched so that there is little doubt about their identity? Or can it be shown that the voices definitely do not match?

The other question we'll take up in this chapter is "What was said?" Imagine trying to understand a recording made of a conversation in a public place, like a bar. Let's say the recording was made by an undercover police agent wearing a wire. It's noisy and there's overtalking. The recording is of lousy quality anyway; cash-strapped police departments don't always have the latest high fidelity equipment. Even with excellent equipment, certain sound frequencies can be lost. In addition to problems understanding what words were said, there can be difficulties understanding what the speakers intended to communicate. Not only do participants tend to be cautious in contexts where they understand that police might like a record of what they say, even in ordinary conversation there are typically differences between the literal meaning and the intended communicative meaning. (Think Grice.) Imperfect understanding caused by these factors can be exacerbated by listener expectations or bias. Some of these factors affect the "who said it?" question as well.

If you're new to linguistics, to make sense of the material in this chapter you'll need to know a little about speech sounds – **phonetics** – and how speech sounds are organized in languages – **phonology.** A short introduction to these areas is provided in the Appendix.

4.1 "Who said it?" Speaker identification

4.1.1 Earwitnesses

A famous case from the 1930s, the kidnapping and murder of Charles Lindbergh's infant son, hinged on identification of a speaker on the basis of his voice alone. Following the kidnapper's instructions, Lindbergh had driven to a cemetery at night to deliver the demanded ransom. Sitting in the car, Lindbergh heard a voice call "Here, Doctor! Over here! Over here!" After some dramatic twists and turns in detective work, a suspect, Richard Bruno Hauptmann, was arrested. Twenty-nine months after hearing the words in the cemetery, Lindbergh heard Hauptmann, in custody, say the same words, and identified Hauptmann as the speaker. At trial, Lindbergh so testified, as an "earwitness," helping convict Hauptmann. Hauptmann was sentenced to death and executed in the electric chair on April 3, 1936. Interestingly, despite pressure, and the inducement of possibly avoiding execution, Hauptmann never confessed.

If the trial were held today, Lindbergh would have been cross-examined about his earwitness testimony more extensively than he apparently was, and both Hauptmann's defense and the prosecution might have addressed issues with earwitness testimony, including the following. People vary in how good they are at recognizing voices. How good was Lindbergh at it? Voices with unusual properties are easier to recognize than ordinary ones. How distinctive was Hauptmann's voice? Hauptmann had a German accent, though how much of one is unclear. Accuracy in identifying voices is much harder when one listens to a voice in a language one doesn't understand, and is harder also when one listens to a dialect different from one's own. Accuracy in recognition diminishes over time; in this case, twenty-nine months had elapsed between Lindbergh's hearing the utterance in the cemetery and his hearing Hauptmann say the same words. Familiarity with a voice can aid recognition considerably, but Lindbergh had heard the voice from the cemetery only that one time. On the other hand, a listener's expectation to hear a particular voice often leads to a mistaken call of identity. All these issues are relevant to "earwitness" testimony.

4.1.2 Spectrograms of voices

The invention of the sound spectrograph in the 1940s was a game-changing technological advance that made possible permanent visual records of sounds, **spectrograms**. Spectrograms display sound amplitude and frequency over time. Examples are shown in (1).

In a spectrogram the horizontal axis represents time; the vertical axis frequency (cycles per second, *aka* "hertz"); and the degree of darkness marks loudness ("amplitude"). The human voice is acoustically complex, with bundles of sound at different frequency levels, observable most obviously in the dark horizontal bands, called **formants**, representing vowels (and vowel-like sounds like the American English syllabic /r/ as in *bird*). In (1), *batch* and *badge* begin identically. They differ in the length of the vowel; the [æ] vowel in *badge* is longer because it precedes the voiced [d]. They differ too

1. a. "batch"   b. "badge"

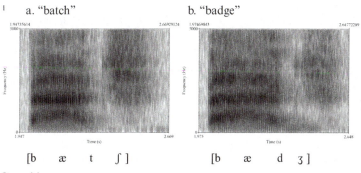

Figure 4.1

in the final consonants; the voicelessness of the [t] can be seen in the absence of acoustic energy in the first and second formants (counting from the bottom up). Contrast the presence of energy for the [d] of *badge*. Both words have an abundance of acoustic energy, not divided among clear formants, for the final fricatives.

To see how the formants look for a different vowel, look at (2):

2   "beach"

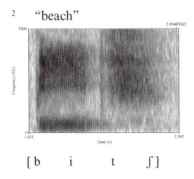

[b   i   t   ʃ]

Figure 4.2

Notice the different shape of the formants for [i] and the big gap between Formant 1 and Formant 2 as contrasted with [æ] above.

4.1.2.1   Spectrograms for speaker identification?

In 1962 a Bell Labs engineer, Lawrence Kersta, published a paper entitled "Voiceprint Identification" enthusing over the potential of spectrograms, which he dubbed "voiceprints," to identify speakers. The idea was that since everybody's voice is unique, spectrograms contained patterns unique to individual speakers. The analog with fingerprints is obvious. Kersta's work reported remarkable accuracy rates in identifying speakers – 99% – achieved by individuals trained in reading spectrograms. Later work, by others, was not so successful. That later work showed that accuracy in identifying speakers based on spectrograms of words pronounced in various phonetic contexts was considerably lower than spectrograms of words spoken in isolation. Moreover, there was variation in accuracy of identification of different speakers, some being easier to identify than others, and it was shown that accuracy can be negatively affected also by non-linguistic factors such as speaker fatigue, emotional stress, and illness.

To get a rough feel for what it's like to visually inspect spectrograms in a search for similarities, try this. Figure 4.3 shows six spectrograms of utterances of the word *bank*. Based on your visual inspection of them, how many speakers do you think produced them? If more than one, try to group any you think were produced by the same speaker. (The answer is at the end of the chapter.)

3   Six spectrograms

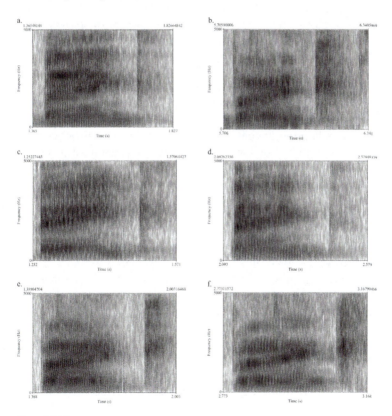

Figure 4.3 Six spectrograms

This exercise suffers from the extremely significant limitation that you don't know anything about how typical or atypical sound features discernible in the spectrograms are in the population from which the spectrograms came. The linguist Geoffrey Morrison (2013) compares the problem to police discovering footprints at a crime scene. In one scenario, the footprints are size ten, and a suspect in custody wears size ten shoes. In another, the footprints are size 14, and the suspect wears size 14. Because size 14 is much rarer than size ten, the size 14 evidence (tending to prove the suspect's guilt) is much more convincing than the size ten evidence (which is hardly relevant at all). In the same way, a pronunciation feature rare in the population used for comparison which occurs in the speech of a suspect is much more valuable for the purpose of speaker identification than a feature common in the relevant population which also occurs in a suspect's speech.

Naturally, the case for identity of the two speakers would increase with additional phonetic features – if they are independent. The independence criterion is important. Suppose both an unknown and a known voice have lots of examples of Chicago-type vowels, for example pronouncing *pot* as [pʰat], with a central rather than back vowel, that is, in a way approaching the pronunciation of *pat* in other American dialects, e.g., [pʰæt], though not going that far, and also lots of examples of pronouncing *pat* in a way approaching "payut" or "peh-yut" in other American dialects (phonetically something like [pʰɛjət]. Both of these pronunciations are typical in the northern midwest (they are manifestations of the **northern cities vowel shift** (Labov, Yeager, & Steiner 1972)). Discovering that the two voices also centralize the vowel in "bed," pronouncing it so its pronunciation approaches that of "bud" in other American dialects, supports the conclusion that both speakers speak the same regional dialect, but since the centralization of the "bed" vowel is another manifestation of the northern cities vowel shift this would provide only a little additional evidence of speaker identity. However, if both speakers also **neutralized** the /ɪ/ – /ɛ/ distinction before nasals, pronouncing *pin* and *pen* identically, but *pit* and *pet* distinctly, that would support speaker identity, since loss of the /

i/ – /ɛ/ distinction is independent of the northern cities vowel shift. (It suggests a southern U.S. speech pattern.)

Back to spectrograms. The term "voiceprint" is misleading, because spectrograms are actually quite different from fingerprints (and DNA, another putative analog). Most phonetic scientists who have considered the term disapprove of it, but it is still used in popular media. Fingerprints and DNA don't change, but a speaker's vocal production of a word is different every time the speaker utters it. Fingerprints and DNA are physical characteristics of individual human beings unaffected by behavior, whereas the phonetic properties of a person's speech are affected by, for example, the speaker's emotional or physical state, aims in speaking, and context. Imagine the effects on your speech of being angry, depressed, drunk, or afraid. And think about how you might speak differently in different contexts: (a) intimately, to a lover, (b) in a conversation with a classmate who you don't know well; (c) to strangers who you want to impress, as in a job interview; (d) using baby-talk to an infant.

Another factor affecting speech form is how attentive a speaker is to their speech. How would you read a list of minimal pairs (*get – gate, god – guard, appear - appeal*)? Probably carefully, because you can't help but attend to the sound differences. Contrast how you might tell a story to a person you're close to about a childhood game you loved, or your experience as a kid being bullied. Speech in such situations shows essentially no effect of attention to the form (e.g., word choice, sentence structure, pronunciation) of speech; instead, speakers focus on the content of their stories.

Besides the sociolinguistic dimensions of within-speaker variability mentioned above, there are differences due to recording conditions. A recording of an unknown speaker might be from a cell phone, with street noise. One of a known speaker might be made in a small room in a police station with echoes from walls. Such recording mismatches can raise the chances of mistakes both of concluding identity and concluding non-identity.

With all this in mind, consider the identification problem in more detail: Imagine a "voice lineup." Suppose you are asked to compare a spectrogram of Person A's speech with spectrograms of (let's say) five unknown speakers. Is one of them Person A? Methodologically, there are two possibilities: (i) you know that one of the five spectrograms is from Person A, and (ii) you don't. Under the much easier condition (i), all you have to do is find the one of the five candidate spectrograms that is most similar to the known spectrogram from Person A. This may not be trivially easy, but it is obviously much easier than under condition (ii). Unfortunately, condition (ii) is much more typical in forensic contexts. Of course, typically the comparison set has just one member, the spectrogram of an unknown speaker who may or may not be Person A, but this could actually make the decision even harder because of the absence of comparison spectrograms.

For comparison to be possible, the known speaker, Person A, needs to utter the same words as the unknown speaker. Barring the rare situation of having a recording of Person A saying those words in unsolicited natural speech – how lucky would that be for law enforcement? – Person A, possibly a suspect in a crime, for example our unhappy employee introduced at the beginning of this chapter, has to utter those words non-spontaneously, and have them recorded. For best results, of course, Person A should produce an utterance as close as possible to the unknown voice in style. The easiest, because it's everybody's default style, is ordinary conversational style. Great, if that is the unknown speaker's style in the recording. If it isn't, accuracy of the mimicry will probably be less. Either way, directly requesting Person A to mimic another voice raises two opposite problems. First, Person A may try to disguise their voice in an effort to differentiate their voice from the unknown sample, leading possibly to a miss – a mistaken conclusion that the voices come from different speakers. Second, an effort to mimic accurately might give rise to a mistaken conclusion that the voices come from the same speaker, a false identification. Not requesting mimicry, that is, just asking Person A to say a particular word or phrase, maybe without hearing the unknown speaker, may work better, but only if the unknown speaker's utterance was in everyday conversational style (rather than a marked style such as angry, excited, or upset).

The claims made by Kersta in his 1962 paper were about visual inspection of spectrograms. Later studies added listening. The combined "aural-spectrographic" approach therefore relied on both listening and expert visual inspection of spectrograms. A spectrogram might provide acoustic information useful for speaker identification not aurally perceptible. The combined method worked better, in the harder situation of words in context, in fact so much better that visual inspection may not have added anything to the accuracy obtainable just aurally, despite the possibility that a spectrogram might contain information that a listener might not pick up.

Whether coupled with listening or done alone, for visual inspection of spectrograms to work reliably, inspectors need to know what aspects of a spectrogram are relevant for speaker identity and how similar these aspects have to be to provide evidence for speaker identity (or how different they have to be to indicate that the voices belong to different speakers). These issues have created something of a gulf between skeptical academic speech scientists on the one hand and, on the other hand, some commercial enterprises, enthusiastic for obvious reasons, and some elements of law enforcement eager for any potentially useful investigative help.

Protocols for visually analyzing spectrograms can look well-grounded:

4   Visual comparison of spectrograms involves, in general, the examination of spectrograph [*sic*] features of like sounds as portrayed in spectrograms in terms of time, frequency and amplitude... Aural cues ... include resonance quality, pitch, temporal factors, inflection, dialect, articulation, syllable grouping, breath pattern disguise, pathologies and other peculiar speech characteristics.

   AFTI (n.d.) Voice Print Identification, Applied Forensic Technologies International, Inc., www.aftiinc.co./voice.htm, cited in Rose 2002. (As of 6/13/18, the link is inoperative.)

But this list of parameters is not accompanied by any mention of what characteristics of the various factors are relevant for speaker comparison, or, more importantly, of what threshold values of degree of similarity, or difference, are empirically justified to provide strong evidence for, or against, speaker identity. The words "are empirically justified" are important. Simply asserting that, say, 10 similar realizations of phonemes is necessary (or sufficient) to establish speaker identity is useless unless there is empirical support for that number.

4.1.2.2   Admissibility of "voiceprints"

Despite these problems, expert analysis of spectrograms for the purpose of speaker identification is still accepted in some U.S. courts. According to the 2018 U.S. Attorney's Criminal Resource Manual § 258, "The majority of the [federal] courts which have considered the question have ruled that voiceprint evidence is admissible."

Three legally operative standards are used in the United States for deciding whether expert testimony should be admitted as evidence in court. The oldest, and least used (in only eight states, and no federal courts), is from a 1923 appellate decision, *Frye v. United States*. The *Frye* standard for admission of expert testimony is this: "[The thing from which the deduction is made must be sufficiently established to have gained general acceptance in the particular field in which it belongs." The Frye standard is therefore sometimes called the "general acceptance" test. While general acceptance in a scientific field excludes new crackpot theories, it also excludes new theories which are scientifically valid but which are too new to have achieved widespread acceptance; and it does not exclude generally accepted *old* theories which newer evidence shows to be wrong.

Frye was overruled for use in federal courts by a 1993 Supreme Court case, *Daubert v. Merrell Dow Pharmaceuticals Inc*. *Daubert* held that general acceptance in a field was not a precondition for admission into evidence. Expert evidence is admissible, according to *Daubert,* if is scientifically valid, i.e., the product of the scientific method: hypothesis formation and empirical testing of the hypothesis. *Daubert* thus replaced the *Frye* "marketplace of scientific ideas" criterion with a look at whether the work was scientifically valid. Most of the states use the *Daubert* standard (as of 2018, 39, plus the District of Columbia). Three states, Nevada, North Dakota, and Virginia, use their own standards, though two of them, Nevada's and Virginia's, are similar to the *Daubert* standard.

The third standard, Rule 702 of the Federal Rules of Evidence (FRE), governs expert testimony in federal courts. An expert may testify if all the following conditions are met:

[5]   (a) the expert's scientific, technical, or other specialized knowledge will help the trier of fact to understand the evidence or to determine a fact in issue;
(b) the testimony is based on sufficient facts or data;
(c) the testimony is the product of reliable principles and methods; and
(d) the expert has reliably applied the principles and methods to the facts of the case.

Federal Rules of Evidence, Rule 702

What actually happened was that *Daubert* held Rule 702, not *Frye*, had to be used in federal courts. *Daubert* can be seen as elaborating what Rule 702 required in terms of scientific reliability: basically, the scientific method.

So how does spectrographic analysis of voices fare under these standards? Despite being generally admissible as evidence, not all that well. A 2003 case, *U.S. v. Angleton*, held that there was "great dispute among researchers and the few practitioners in the field over the accuracy and reliability of voice spectrographic analysis... [T]he error rates...are unknown and vary widely depending on the conditions under which the analysis was made."

Nonetheless, police detecting and crime prevention, free from the high standard courts require because they don't need proof, just probability, can use spectrograms to include or exclude a person from set of suspects.

4.1.3 Linguistic analysis

Probably the best-known example of the use of linguistic analysis, as opposed to acoustic phonetics, to answer the "Who said it?" question is sociolinguist William Labov's analysis and testimony in a 1987 bomb threat case. Here's how Labov summarized his contribution, in a 2013 interview with Gregory Guy, a sociolinguist himself and former student of Labov's:

6   Bomb threats were being made to the Pan American company. And some executives at Pan American said that the voice sounded like Paul Prinzivalli, who was considered a disgruntled employee. He was arrested and spent 9 months in prison, insisting he was innocent. The UCLA phonetics lab sent me recordings of the bomb threats and the prisoner saying the same words, and it was immediately evident that he was innocent! The bomb threats were made by a speaker with a Boston accent, and Prinzivalli was a clear New Yorker. The people from Los Angeles who had misidentified him were unfamiliar with East Coast dialects. So I was able to testify as an expert witness in a way that went beyond just giving an opinion, but presenting facts that were so clear that the judge in deciding the case – acquitting Prinzivalli – paid tribute to the objectivity of the linguistic evidence. So that made it clear to me that the law is looking for objective evidence. Lots of times we give testimony that is only an opinion. But in any case where you have evidence that demonstrate facts that must be true, you're doing the law a great favor.

Guy 2013

Labov saw his challenge as finding ways to convince a west coast court, whose knowledge of phonetics and phonology was nil, and whose knowledge of American dialectology was probably limited to vague impressions of "eastern" and "southern" "accents," that phonetic, phonological, and dialectological facts inescapably led to the conclusion that Prinzivalli was innocent. In other words, Labov did not want simply to opine; he wanted to teach the judge enough basic linguistics for the scientific facts to persuade him. Linguistics is not an overwhelmingly technical science, but what it is about is unfamiliar to most people (contrast, say, chemistry or geology), and the fundamentals of phonetics – especially acoustic phonetics – and phonology are both forbidding and snooze-inducing to most people. So Labov's teaching problem was tough and he had to get it right; a person's freedom depended on it.

Labov showed the judge that the threat caller and Prinzivalli had different phonemic systems, specifically in the vowels in the words *bomb* and *off* used in the threat calls. The sound systems of most Americans in roughly the eastern third of the country distinguish these vowels, using /ɑ/ – a low back unrounded vowel – in *bomb* and /ɔ/– a mid back round vowel – in *off.* The Boston dialect is an exception. There, the two sounds have merged into one, so words like *Don* and *dawn* are pronounced identically (as are *cot* and *caught* and *hottie* and *haughty* and other pairs). The threat caller pronounced *bomb* and *off* in the Boston way, using the same vowel – phonetic symbol [ɒ], a low back round vowel – in both, and Prinzivalli pronounced those words in the New York way, using a low back unrounded vowel, [ɑ], in *bomb*, and a mid-back rounded vowel, [ɔ], in *off.* Labov played a recording of one of the threat calls and a recording of Prinzivalli saying the same words through very high quality speakers so that the judge, a west coast dialect speaker, was able to hear clearly the pronunciation difference. But Labov went further, presenting charts summarizing the differences between the threat caller's Boston sound system and Prinzivalli's New York system, and including other words that pattern like *bomb* and *off* in the two dialects so the judge could see the systematic pattern of which the pronunciations of *bomb* and *off* were just one example. Labov also showed that the caller's pronunciation of *that* in "I hope you're on that" marked him as a Bostonian. New York City English has [æ] in *that* whereas in Boston speech that word has the same vowel ([ɛjᵊ]) as in *there* (*there* has [ɛjᵊ] in both dialects). In fact, the bomb threat caller's *that* was initially mistranscribed as *there,* in the sentence "I hope you're on that." (The final /t/ was unreleased, making it hard to notice when played through mediocre speakers, but it was audible when Labov played the recording through his high quality speakers.)

The judge had Prinzivalli say the pledge of allegiance to the flag, and asked if Labov could point to specific features of Prinzivalli's pronunciations that marked him as a New Yorker. Labov showed that Prinzivalli had the typical New York City pronunciations of *flag, stands,* and *all:* [ɛjᵊ]) in *flag* and *stands,* and [ɔ] in *all.* The [ɛjᵊ]) vowel always occurs before voiced stops in New York City, distinguishing New York City English from neighboring varieties such as Philadelphia English: In New York, but not elsewhere, [ɛjᵊ]) occurs before /g/.

On cross-examination, Labov was asked whether a New Yorker could successfully imitate a Boston dialect. Sounds plausible, right? It's actually quite difficult. Even stereotypical pronunciations can be hard for a mimic to get right. When I lived in Australia, I once tried to sound Australian over the phone with a stranger, a government official, by dropping my preconsonantal and word-final /r/s and turning my American /ej/ vowel (as in *Taylor*) into the corresponding Australian sound, something close to [aj] (Aussies pronounce *main* almost the way Americans pronounce *mine*). I gave my address to the official, *45 Taylor Street,* dropping the /r/ s in *forty* and *Taylor,* and adjusting the vowels in *five, Taylor,* and *Street* to what I thought would be accurate mimicry of Australian pronunciation. I failed. After a pause, the official asked me, exaggerating the different vowels, "Is that *Taylor* or *Tyler* street?"

When speakers try, they may get certain well-known features more or less right, or may not, as in the example above, but it is especially hard to mimic accurately features that are below the level of conscious awareness. In an article about his work on the case, Labov wrote the following:

7　　If it could be shown that the defendant had a long familiarity with the Boston dialect, and a great talent for imitation, then one could not rule out the possibility that he has done a perfect reproduction of the Boston system. But if so, he would have accomplished a feat that had not yet been reported for anyone else.

Labov 1988,180

After the prosecutor's closing arguments, it was the defense's turn. The judge intervened and said it was unnecessary. He acquitted Prinzivalli. Prinzivalli had by then spent 15 months in jail and had refused – about halfway through that period - to accept a prosecution offer of a sentence of time served in exchange for a guilty plea.

4.2 What was said

Usually when a recording is evidence for what was said, the jury gets to hear it. After all, members of the jury understand spoken English and are as competent as anyone else to understand what was said. This is different from speaker identification, in which similar-sounding voices might – theoretically, notwithstanding all the problems raised above – be found identical, or distinguished, through scientific evidence like spectrographic analysis.

4.2.1 What were the words?

Some of the same problems that afflict determining speaker identity also affect understanding what was said. A recorded speaker's emotional or physical state can affect intelligibility. Ambient noise - was the recording made in a noisy bar? – or recording deficiencies – was the recording made of a phone call? – raises obvious difficulties. Listener expectation or bias is a big problem too. In our adversarial judicial system, one side has a recording. It's far from unusual for that side's interpretation of the tape to be affected by that side's expectations or hopes. Naturally the same thing happens when the other side listens to the same tape.

Phonetically reduced syllables can be a source of mistakes. A case in which Roger Shuy was involved hinged on the location of unstressed –n't in a tag question:

8   Wrong prosecution transcription:
      I would take a bribe, wouldn't you?

I wouldn't take a bribe, would you?

Shuy, testifying as an expert, showed the jury, by having them count the beats, that the recorded utterance had a brief but noticeable pause after six syllables, not five:

9   I would n't take a bribe   would you
     1   2   3   4 5 6   Pause

Shuy 2011

Noticing the location of the pause made it clear that the negation attached to the first *would*.

A significant danger of mistake comes from the use of transcripts given to the jury. Even when listeners hear a recording while reading a transcript of its words, they tend to place undue reliance on the transcript. If the recording is of less than stellar quality the tendency to believe the transcript is stronger, and even if it is stellar, people tend to believe the transcript. Linguist Ellen Prince worked as an expert hired by the defense in several federal cases. After listening to tapes recorded by the FBI, she found an average of 14 important errors per page in the transcripts. Here's one of her examples ("T" is an undercover police officer wearing a wire, "D" the defendant in the case):

10   Wrong FBI transcription:

   T: [discussion of FBI investigation and own fears]
   D: Jesus Christ - that's a shame. I don't know what the hell to do.

   Accurate transcription:

   T: [discussion of FBI investigation and own fears] [4 sec.]
   D: Jesus Christ. [5 sec.] That's a shame. [3 sec.] I don't know what the hell to tell you.

Prince 1990, 282

The FBI's rendition has "D" clearly pursuing his own interests, whereas the accurate transcription has him responding to what T has said in a more detached way.

Sometimes a transcript omits utterances as "non-pertinent" which actually matter. Here's another example from Prince:

11   Wrong FBI transcription:

> D: Just watch them. Don't do, don't let them know too much of your business – believe me. They are treacherous motherfuckers, I tell you. And I know dealing with freight, they're no good, they'll beat you to death. *(Non-pertinent conversation.)*

Accurate transcription:

> D: Just watch them. Don't do it, don't let them know too much of your business, believe me. They're treacherous motherfuckers, I'll tell you. And I know with dealing with freight, they're no good, they beat you to death. You give them fucking gold, they come back with the price of copper.

Id. 282

The FBI transcription can easily be taken as a warning about actual physical violence. The accurate transcription includes the metaphor of "gold" vs. "the price of copper," clarifying that what is being said is not a literal statement about physical violence, just a figure of speech about price.

4.2.2 What did the speaker mean by the words?

When prosecutors or plaintiffs try to prove someone's guilt or liability from the person's words, typically the argument – or the assumption – is that the person's saying the words meant that the person was committed to the truth of the proposition the words represent. This assumption fits our ordinary assumptions about communication and is often accurate. If you ask somebody a factual question about the time of day or the weather or what they're planning to do during the weekend, in the normal course of events they reply truthfully, and just about always you EXPECT them to. Grice's Quality maxim, "Try to tell the truth," captures this expectation. However, a fair bit of ordinary conversation is carried out NOT in accord with the assumption. As a blanket assumption it's wrong.

First, people say literally untrue things to be sarcastic ("Oh, you're a fine friend!" to a friend who has betrayed the friendship), hyperbolic ("I was literally freezing to death" when the speaker felt cold), or metaphorical ("Prof. Wye's class is a zoo"). Then there are polite lies like declining an invitation with a false excuse, for example, turning down an unwelcome date request by saying "I have other plans." The plausibility of having other plans lessens the hurt of the rejection; contrast "No thanks, you're not my type."

Here's an example of possible polite lies, again from Ellen Prince. In the conversation below, "T" is an assistant chief of police wearing a wire, "D" a police chief under investigation in a bribery case. The issue was whether D knew about other police officers' taking bribes. T makes strenuous efforts to elicit an incriminating statement from D. Immediately before D's first utterance below, T has gone through a long conversational turn expressing his fears about his own criminal liability. There follows a long (8 second) pause, one of several after utterances by T. Finally, D responds:

12   D: I'll tell you, they certainly have created a monster… [10 sec.] You just uh…[4 sec.] You didn't do anything else–anything wrong o–other than what: everybody else on the police force did at that time. At Christmas time, we accepted//

T: //Oh man! Christmas time, it was like–I remember the days, Christmas time used to be like//
D: //Damn right. Christmas time, everybody accepted money.

Id., 285

(The mark "//" represents simultaneous talk, "overtalk.") When D testified at trial, his explanation of his apparently incriminating statements was that he was trying to calm T down. Part of his testimony was "I thought that was what he wanted to hear." He testified that he had no specific knowledge of any police officers receiving improper gifts. Maybe, maybe not, but his explanation is at least plausible, perhaps especially given T's possibly manipulative use of silences. Prince's comment: "Silence is painfully unacceptable in social conversation and often inspires speakers to take desperate measures." Silence can also represent a speaker's uncertainty about what to say, or an invitation for one's conversational partner to speak. Taking D's account as accurate, in D's first utterance above, his 10 second silence seems to represent his hope that T would take up the conversational burden. When T doesn't, D's "You just uh..." leads to another (4 second) stretch of silence, again an invitation for T to play his conversational part, again silently declined. Finally, D gives T what he thinks T wants, which seems an accurate guess given T's immediate enthusiastic agreement, with which D concurs, perhaps partly to protect T's positive face. The point is not that D's explanation and the above analysis of the conversation is necessarily what actually happened; for all we know, D might be guilty, and his utterances are evidence of it. Rather, the point is that conversational behavior like that of D under his account of it is plausible because it is the kind of thing that occurs in conversation all the time, and it's a mistake for anyone (for example, police, attorneys, jurors, judges) to believe otherwise.

Along similar lines are **back channel cues** like "yeah," "uh huh," "OK," and the like, which can signal something like "I understand what you are saying," rather than "I agree." Replying with one or another of these can protect the addressee's positive face by communicating that one is paying attention. It can happen, though, that utterances like these are introduced into trial evidence to show the speaker's agreement with some proposition. As above, these CAN communicate assent or agreement; the point is that their other use, the back channel one, is entirely normal and common. Here's an example from a case I was involved in. The conversation is between "UC," an undercover police officer, and "D," the defendant, who was charged with smuggling drugs into a prison and delivering them to an inmate named Destiny. UC has introduced the topic of exchanging an envelope containing money for one containing drugs. ("Ohs" means "ounces.")

13 UC: I like make sure, you know what I mean? I no can go short and the they frickin come back on me uh?
D: Yeah.

...

UC: For Destiny. OK, so that's the two ohs then.
D: OK.
UC. OK.
D: I guess. I don't know.
UC: OK.
D: (Laughs)

In this stretch of conversation, D's first utterance, "Yeah," is ambiguous between meaning "I agree" and "I understand; go on," an ambiguity without much significance because "I agree" here conveys only agreement with UC's hypothetical. In contrast, D's second utterance, "OK," is ambiguous in a way that matters; it could signal D's agreement with UC's proposition that the envelope in question would contain the two "ohs" for Destiny, an interpretation very bad for D. Alternatively, it could just be a back channel cue meaning "I understand; go on." D's next utterance, the non-committal "I guess. I don't know," conveys (truly or falsely) D's detachment from the content of UC's utterances about drugs and money, consistent with the back channel cue interpretation of his previous "OK."

4.2.3 Significant silence – or not

Remember **adoptive admissions** from Chapter 3? The adoptive admission rule allows in, as evidence in a trial, a person's silence in the context of a utterance by someone else implying the person's guilt for a crime, and allows a jury to decide whether the person's silence was a tacit admission.

In Chapter 3, factors favoring silence were mentioned, including not hearing or understanding an accusation, not finding it important (contrast these utterances from a spouse: "You forgot to take out the trash" and "You have been unfaithful to me"), not wanting to dignify an outrageous accusation with a response, feeling too intimidated to speak up, and not wanting to incriminate someone else.

Courts vary in their acceptance of adoptive admissions. Ainsworth 2011 cites examples of courts' accepting them: A corporate executive was asked by a reporter whether he had been "cooking the books." The executive replied "Next question." The court found that a "reasonable man," if innocent, would have responded specifically in the negative. (Really? Always?) In another case cited by Ainsworth, a defendant told an accuser to "shut the fuck up." The appellate court found this reply insufficiently responsive and took it as an admission of guilt. (Again: Really?) Ainsworth's comment is that such behavior by judges assumes a "caricature of discursive behavior."

4.3 Conclusion

In this chapter we have explored issues involving recorded speech and other out-of-court speech behavior (the silence in adoptive admissions). Approaches to speaker identification – the "Who said it?" question – included acoustic phonetics (spectrographic analysis) and linguistic structure (phonology and dialectology). Approaches to content discovery – the "What was said?" question – included applications of phonetics and phonology (e.g., Shuy's syllable-and-pause analysis), just plain careful, disinterested listening (as in Prince's examples of repairing mis-transcriptions by law enforcement), and interactional analysis involving, among other things, politeness considerations and Gricean implicature.

Next on the agenda: crimes of language.

ANSWER to speaker identification exercise, ex. (3): There are two speakers, each the source of three spectrograms. One speaker produced spectrograms (a), (c), and (d), the other (b), (e), and (f).

Each speaker pronounced the word *bank* in isolation, sentence-finally in a Yes–No question (*Did she rob the bank?*), and sentence-medially in a non-stressed position in a *wh*-question (*Which bank do you prefer?*). Specifically:

Spectrogram (a): Speaker A, sentence-final.
Spectrogram (b): Speaker B, sentence-final.
Spectrogram (c): Speaker A, sentence-medial.
Spectrogram (d): Speaker A, isolation.
Spectrogram (e): Speaker B, isolation.
Spectrogram (f): Speaker B, sentence-medial.

Chapter 5

Crimes of language (and one tort)

5.0 Introduction

Your buddy Frankie has been charged with burglary. At his trial, you testify in his defense that he spent the whole evening when the burglary occurred at your apartment with you watching TV. You are lying, but it's in a good cause; he's a good guy, and if he goes to prison again, you are certain it will be for a long time and will probably ruin his life. Unfortunately, the prosecutors show that Frankie could not have been at your place, because they have three credit card slips, signed undeniably by Frankie, time-marked for the time you testified he was at your apartment. There's also an eyewitness identification. Not only does Frankie go away for several years, you are charged with **perjury**, lying under oath.

When you were a freshman in college, you were dismayed to learn that your high school tormenter, Johnny, was a classmate. You hated the guy, with good reason. He was a social leader. He took advantage of his popularity and way with words to tease and bully you mercilessly, and you, pretty much a nerd, did not handle it well. When you got to college, you were unhappy to see that he was not only at your college, but even in one of your classes. You told your roommate the whole story, and, OK, you embellished it with some made-up stories that Johnny had had arrests for shoplifting. The false stories spread. When Johnny got wind of the stories, he had no trouble tracing them back to you. Oops. Johnny sued you for

defamation, publicly making statements which the speaker knows are false and which damage someone's reputation.

Some crimes are linguistic by nature. **Perjury** always is. The same goes for **defamation** (except it's not a crime, but a **tort**, a wrongful act which a person can be sued for). **Soliciting** someone to commit a crime and **conspiracy**, being involved in the joint planning of a crime, just about have to be performed linguistically. Some crimes can be carried out non-linguistically as well as by language, like **bribery** and **threatening**, but since they crucially involve communication, it's possible to make the same kind of analysis for them as for purely linguistic acts. In this chapter we'll look in turn at perjury, defamation, solicitation, and conspiracy.

5.1 Perjury

Lying isn't a crime generally, but if you lie under oath in a legal proceeding (like a trial), it is, IF your lie is about a **material** matter. If you testify falsely that you have a cold when your cough really comes from nervousness, you'll probably get away with it, but you might not if you falsely deny having a fresh $50,000 in your bank account if you're on trial for embezzling. So first: what is a lie?

5.1.1 What is a lie?

According to an influential 1981 paper by linguists Linda Coleman and Paul Kay, a prototypical lie has three elements: (i) a false proposition which (ii) the speaker believes to be false, uttered with (iii) the intent to deceive. To these could be added a requirement that a lie be accomplished by an **assertion,** rather than any other speech act, ruling out from the denotation of *lie* questions, exclamatives ("What a great party!"), and imperatives. A parent who tells their rebellious teenager "Take out the trash" won't hear back from the teenager anything like "That's a lie!" The "assertion" requirement also rules out false presuppositions, so saying "I'm glad the Yankees won last night" when they actually lost renders *The Yankees won last night* inside the bigger sentence not a lie; on the other hand, the whole statement, including the "I'm glad…" part, IS – probably – a lie, because it's not possible to be glad about a nonexistent state of affairs. The "probably" hedge is needed to rule out mistakes. If the speaker mistakenly believed the Yankees won last night, the statement is not a lie.

Omitted from Coleman & Kay's *lie* characteristics was reprehensibility. The idea is that reprehensibility is a cultural fact, not a linguistic one. Cultures differ in how they view the goodness or badness of asserting different kinds of untruths. When I lived in Tanzania, my housemate and I invited a couple of Tanzanians we had met to dinner at our house. They agreed to come at six the next evening. We prepared a nice dinner. Our new Tanzanian friends never showed up. Several days later we encountered one of them at the market and asked him what happened. The reply, a bemused "Oh, I went to Dar es Salaam," made clear that his agreeing to come to dinner had been no more than a polite response that was not intended to convey a commitment. My housemate and I had been put out by their not showing up and then not apologizing, but we had to chalk the episode up to a cross-cultural misunderstanding.

5.1.2 Implicating an untruth

Before getting back to perjury, consider one more example:

1   Quentin: Do you have a Tesla?
    Ann: I have a Honda Civic.

Suppose Ann has both a Honda Civic and a Tesla. Under Coleman & Kay's schema, Ann has presumably said something true that she believes true, uttered with the intent to deceive. From a Gricean perspective, her answer is true in the literal sense, false in its implicature, namely, that she doesn't have a Tesla. The operative Gricean maxim is Relevance. This maxim says simply "Be relevant," in Grice's original formulation, but later work (in the approach known as **Relevance Theory** (see, e.g., Sperber & Wilson 1995)) strengthens the maxim to "Maximize relevance." Ann's answer is relevant, because it is about the make of car that she drives, which is part of what Quentin wants to know. But her answer would have been much more relevant if she had responded specifically to what was asked. A maximally relevant answer would have been "Yep, but (*or:* and) I also have a Honda Civic."

Back to perjury. Here's the federal perjury statute:

2   Whoever…having taken an oath before a competent tribunal… that he will testify…truly…, willfully and contrary to such oath states…any material matter which he does not believe to be true…is guilty of perjury…

18 U.S.C. § 1621

Interestingly, the perjury statute includes only one of the three of Coleman & Kay's *lie* elements, but it's the most important one, not believing one's statement.

Consider the following (true) story. You'll see that it's similar to Quentin and Ann's little conversation above. A man named Samuel Bronston had a movie production company. It made movies in several foreign countries and had bank accounts in some of them. In one year it had 37 accounts in five different countries. After one of the company's movies was a bust, the company filed for bankruptcy. At a hearing, creditors wanted to know about overseas assets. The following exchange took place between an attorney for the creditors and Bronston:

3   Q. Do you have any bank accounts in Swiss banks, Mr. Bronston?
     A. No, sir.
     Q. Have you ever?
     A. The company had an account there for about six months, in Zurich.

Bronston v. U.S., 409 U.S. 352 (1973)

The facts were that Bronston had had a Swiss bank account into and out of which a lot of money had moved ($180,000, a lot today, but a great deal more in purchasing power at the time). Bronston had closed this account just before the hearing. So his first answer was true, because at the time of the hearing, he did not have any accounts in Swiss banks. Now look at his second answer. It turns out this answer was also true; the company had had, for about six months, one or more Swiss bank accounts. But this answer was not – literally – an answer to the question the attorney had asked. It *was* an answer, though, in its implicature that Bronston himself had never had a Swiss bank account. A *false* answer.

Did Bronston's answer violate the federal statute given above in (2)? Did he "state a material matter which he did not believe to be true?" He certainly *communicated* one. Let's distinguish the two interpretations, calling one "literal" and the other "implicated." (And let's assume too that Bronston did not make an innocent mistake, that is, he knew what he was doing in his answer.) The table below applies Coleman & Kay's three elements to Bronston's second answer under the two interpretations:

[4]	BELIEVE FALSE	INTENT TO DECEIVE	FALSE
Literal interpretation	-	+	-
Implicated interpretation	+	+	+

Under Coleman and Kay's scheme, what Bronston said was very much a lie in the implicated interpretation, but in the literal interpretation, an utterance with only a small bit of lie-ness to it.

Bronston was charged with perjury. At trial, the jury was instructed that he could be convicted for giving an answer which was "not literally false but when considered in the context in which it was given, nevertheless constitute[d] a false statement." The jury struggled with applying this instruction to Bronston's testimony, requesting clarification and a repetition of the instructions, but ultimately returned a verdict of guilty.

Bronston appealed and lost, 2-1. The Second Circuit Court of Appeals, implicitly following Grice, held that "an answer containing half of the truth which also constitutes a lie by negative implication, when the answer is intentionally given in place of

the responsive answer called for by a proper question, is perjury"
(*U.S. v. Bronston*, 453 F.2d 555, 559 (2d Cir. 1971)).

The dissenting judge wrote

5   [O]nce testimony is found truthful there can be no perjury con-
     viction .., and the jury is not entitled to consider whether the
     defendant hoped that a truthful answer would be interpreted in
     any particular way. Whether Bronston's answer was calculated
     to mislead the questioner and frustrate the bankruptcy
     proceedings should not here concern us...[This may put] a
     burden on the questioner to recognize when he is being led
     astray, but I prefer to insist upon the questioner's acuity than
     to distort the statute. Had [he] noticed that Bronston's answer
     was unresponsive and questioned him with particularity about
     his personal accounts, and had Bronston thereupon answered
     responsively, I suspect that no one would think his original
     unresponsive answer perjurious. Bronston's conviction should
     in no degree depend on the [questioner's] failure to notice he
     was being diverted.

                                                              Id.

Bronston appealed to the Supreme Court. Before I tell you what
happened there, what do you think should have happened? The trial
court jury and appellate court two-judge majority implicitly applied
important facts that we know about communication, facts made
explicit by Grice. The appellate dissent took as more important
what the speaker literally *said* rather than what he implicated, in the
courtroom context. Which analysis seems more persuasive? If you
were a Supreme Court justice, which way would you vote?

Here's the reveal: Bronston won at the Supreme Court, in a
unanimous decision. Chief Justice Burger's opinion distinguished
ordinary conversation from testimony:

6   There is, at the outset, a serious literal problem in applying
     § 1621 to petitioner's answer. The words of the statute con-
     fine the offense to the witness who "willfully ... states ... any
     material matter which he does not believe to be true." Beyond

question, petitioner's answer to the crucial question was not responsive … There is, indeed, an implication in the answer to the second question that there was never a personal bank account; in casual conversation, this interpretation might reasonably be drawn. But we are not dealing with casual conversation, and the statute does not make it a criminal act for a witness to willfully state any material matter that implies any material matter that he does not believe to be true.

Bronston v. United States, 409 U.S. 352, 357–358 (1973)

Burger went on:

[7] It is the responsibility of the lawyer to probe; testimonial interrogation, and cross-examination in particular, is a probing, prying, pressing form of inquiry. If a witness evades, it is the lawyer's responsibility to recognize the evasion and to bring the witness back to the mark, to flush out the whole truth with the tools of adversary examination.

Id., at 358–359.

The Bronston decision, from 1973, is the law today. For perjury, it is only a witness's *statement* that matters, not its implicature.

As Solan and Tiersma point out (2005:215), the "literal truth" defense that *Bronston* authorizes is not available for other crimes involving language; the perpetrator of a holdup carried out by saying "You'd hate it if I shot you" would produce hilarity (and all else being equal, a conviction) if he or she argued that that utterance was not a threat but just a true statement.

The *Bronston* rule's being the law does not guarantee that it's right. Nor does it ensure that the rule is sufficiently clear. It is fair to wonder, for example, what would happen under this doctrine with other instances of implicature, for example, a hyperbolic metaphor: A witness describes an assault and battery by saying "He was killing him." He wasn't; the puny attacker was flailing away ineffectually at a big strong guy who was just fending off the punches. The witness exaggerates to make clear how vicious and violent the (puny, ineffectual) battery was. While the legal definition of battery is "any unwanted touching," a very violent battery is more likely to result in conviction than a tap on someone's shoulder. So the implicature of violence might be considered a "material" matter, under the definition of perjury (given in (2) above). Was the witness's statement "He was killing him" perjury, under the "literal assertion, not implicature" doctrine announced in *Bronston*? Probably not, perhaps because with familiar metaphors nobody notices that the literal meaning is actually different from the conveyed metaphorical meaning. The witness's testimony is understood as meaning "He was attacking him violently." But we don't know; this is not what *Bronston* says.

How about an abuse of the maxim of Quantity, in a different way from Bronston's testimony? Suppose Eddie Embezzler is asked how much money he has in his checking account. He answers, "$5,000." He actually has $50,000 in there. Did he lie? He does have $5,000 in his checking account – along with a lot more. Justice Burger's opinion recognized the interpretive problem and offered a solution:

8   Whether an answer is true must be determined with reference to the question it purports to answer, not in isolation.

Id., footnote 3

But astute as this observation is, it's not how Burger ruled. Does Justice Burger's insistence (in (7) above) that the cross-examining attorney probe and follow up work? One can imagine a near-endless series of questions and answers like this:

9   Q: Any more?
     A: I have $5,500.
     Q: Any more?
     A: I have $6,000.
     Q: Any more?
     A: I have $6,500.
     …

To be sure, the attorney could short-circuit this nonsense by asking for *total* amount in Eddie's checking account. The point is that it is reasonable to use ordinary (Gricean) expectations in order to understand what a witness says, but it's also reasonable to treat testimony as requiring heightened awareness of the possibilities for false implicature. The problem is where and on what basis to draw the line between letting attorneys understand witness' statements normally and requiring them to apply extra vigilance.

One step toward solving this dilemma is to remember the importance of the maxim of Relevance. The most relevant answer to the question "How much money is in your checking account" is the total amount. Because we assume (maximum) relevance from our interlocutors, a surreptitious violation of the Relevance maxim can easily go unnoticed even by the most alert questioner: In the following example, should the attorney be expected to follow up as he or she does?

10   Q: Are you married?
     A: Yes, I've been married to my wife Helene for fifteen years.
     Q: Do you have any spouses currently in addition to Helene?

Examples (9) and (10) are different from the exchange in *Bronston,* where the questioning attorney should have noticed the non-responsiveness – the irrelevance – of Bronston's answer. Testimony like Bronston's (3) can be distinguished from (9) and (10) in the following way: in Bronston's the non-responsiveness is, if not strikingly obvious, at least noticeable, whereas in ((9)) and (10) it isn't. If an answer violates Relevance in an obvious way, the attorney should be obligated to follow up, but if the violation is hidden, that's too much to expect.

A reasonable revision of the federal perjury statute might be along these lines:

11   New definition of perjury

     Perjury occurs when a witness makes a statement that is material (i.e., Relevant!) to the case that he or she does not believe, *or* believes it but knows that the answer, while literally true, implicates something materially false, *and* which appears to responds fully Relevantly to the question but does not.

The formulation in (11) would require judges and attorneys to understand the term *implicates*, but never mind that; a definition could be added in. Under this interpretation, Bronston would get off, as he ultimately did; his response noticeably did not respond maximally Relevantly to the question asked. But neither Eddie ((9)) nor the witness in example (10) would, if the questioning ceased after their first responses – in the latter case, that is, if the fact was that the witness was a bigamist. Both responses were literally true, and they appeared to be fully Relevant but weren't.

5.2 Defamation

Let's return to the story about you and your tormentor Johnny, about whom who you spread nasty rumors that you knew were false. They're obviously damaging to Johnny's reputation. Johnny sues you for **slander**, spoken defamation (written defamation is **libel**).

Defamation is generally governed by state, not federal, law, although there is a federal definition (28 U.S. C. § 4101). Defamation is a **tort**, or civil wrong, for which a person can be sued, rather than a crime. (Even though about a third of the states do have criminal defamation statutes, they are almost never enforced.) The California libel statute is typical:

12   Libel is a false and unprivileged publication by writing, printing, picture, effigy, or other fixed representation to the eye, which exposes any person to hatred, contempt, ridicule, or obloquy, or which causes him to be shunned or avoided, or which has a tendency to injure him in his occupation.

Cal. Civ. Code § 45

We can use this statute as a useful starting point, since it includes all the basic elements of defamation in any jurisdiction. First, notice that a defamatory utterance has to be false. Truth is a sure defense. Next, the definition has a couple of words that might need explanation, "unprivileged" and "exposes." Taking "exposes" first, the idea is that defamation always involves an audience wider than the target; you can't be sued for defamation for criticizing an individual to their face in a one-on-one conversation. As for "unprivileged," the idea is that some communications that might be defamation aren't, if certain conditions are met. For instance, a trial witness is "privileged" to testify to all manner of bad things about somebody without running the risk of a lawsuit for slander. Legislators' utterances made during legislative debate are likewise "privileged." These are **absolute privileges**, protecting from defamation lawsuits even utterances made when the speaker knows they are false. There are also **qualified** privileges, which protect a speaker who makes a false statement but has a good-faith reason to think it's true, for example if they heard it from someone who they reasonably thought was honest and had good reason to say what they said. Example: A reporter includes in a news story an allegation by Walt Wealthy that Walt's bookkeeper embezzled money from him. Walt's allegation is false. But the reporter is protected by the qualified privilege because he or she knows Walt and has always found him honest.

Note that you, the alleged slanderer of Johnny, are in trouble. You have "published" – i.e., disseminated – your claims; they are false (and you know it); and you have neither variety of privilege.

What about expressing, publicly, an *opinion* that hurts someone's reputation: they need to diet, have lousy taste in clothes, or can't carry a tune? Pure opinions, not being statements of fact, are pretty safe. Does this mean that instead of making up lies about specific events, you could get away with it if what you said about Johnny is "In my opinion, Johnny is a kleptomaniac."? Probably not. Just prefacing a statement with "In my opinion,…" or "I think…" won't necessarily protect a person from losing a defamation lawsuit. A 1990 Supreme Court opinion distinguished the possibly defamatory utterance in (a) below from the non-defamatory one in (b):

13   a. In my opinion Mayor Jones is a liar.
       b. In my opinion Mayor Jones shows his abysmal ignorance by accepting the teachings of Marx and Lenin.

Milkovich v. Lorain Journal, 497 U.S. 1 (1990)

The Court drew the distinction by requiring that for defamation an utterance must be "provably false." (14b) isn't, because it's the speaker's judgment call that accepting Marxism demonstrates abysmal ignorance. (14a) is, even though it starts "In my opinion...," because it is presumably empirically determinable whether Mayor Jones is a liar, and that's (again, presumably) the point of the speaker saying what they said. So speakers can get away with expressing "opinions" which aren't provable, like *needs to diet, has lousy taste in clothes,* or *can't carry a tune,* but not opinions like *is a kleptomaniac,* because that's empirically provable.

Look again at the definition in (12). Notably missing is anything about the speaker's intent. Instead the focus is on harm to the reputation of the person who is the target of the speech. In light of this, imagine that in a letter you write to your student newspaper criticizing obnoxious professors, you invent a fictitious Professor Dick Head who one day got so angry at a student who, a minute before class started, was reading the student newspaper, that he threw an eraser at her. It was just a story you made up to satirize mean faculty members. Unfortunately, it turns out that there actually is a professor named Richard Head at your school, and he thinks your letter is about him. So do lots of other members of the college community. When Prof. Head sues you, you are in real trouble: You knew your story was false, it has been disseminated, and it presumably hurts Prof Head's reputation. You are in trouble even though you had no bad intent at all and your carelessness really amounted only to your choice of name ("Ima Scheisskopf" might have been wiser).

In an influential 1987 article, Peter Tiersma suggests equating defamation with "public accusation." Doing so puts us squarely in the domain of speech act theory.

The felicity conditions for the speech act of accusing are presumably these:

14 Felicity conditions for accusing

Semantic content: Past or present act A done by a specific
person or entity X, or act A for which
X is responsible; or past or present
characteristic C of X

Preparatory conditions:	(i) Speaker knows about act A or characteristic C; (ii) Speaker has evidence that act A occurred /is occurring, or that X has characteristic C; (iii) Speaker assumes that addressee does not know about X's act A or characteristic C; (iv) Speaker presupposes act A or characteristic C is bad.
Essence:	Counts as speaker's attributing responsibility for act A to X, or as expressing proposition that C is or was a characteristic of X.

Preparatory condition (iii) is for accusations about a person made to another. It's absent from the felicity conditions for accusations about a person made to that person. An often-useful test to identify an utterance as carrying out a particular illocutionary act is trying to paraphrase the utterance in performative form, using a performative verb, and, optionally, the modifier *hereby*. If someone says "I'll bring the wine," it's a promise if it's paraphrasable as "I (hereby) promise to bring the wine." If the utterance is an offer, a different paraphrase works ("I (hereby) offer to bring the wine."). If someone tells you "That rock is slippery," it's a warning if the utterance can be paraphrased "I warn you: that rock is slippery." If someone yells "Get away from my car," the paraphrase showing it's an order is "I (hereby) order you to get away from my car."

How does this test work for accusations? Satisfactorily for some, but not all. Suppose you discover that your valuable watch is missing from your dorm room, where your classmate Jean was fifteen minutes ago. You tell the campus cops you suspect her. When the officers bring her and you together, she's acting so weird you become convinced she's the thief, and you blurt to the cops "She took my watch!" This can be paraphrased "I accuse her of taking my watch." Often, though, accusations are expressed indirectly. Tiersma gives a (real) example of a presuppositional accusation in a question, "How did you set the fire?", asked by an insurance agent whose addressee was a policyholder whose house had burned down. This can't be paraphrased with a performative, but the content and context made clear that the utterance had the illocutionary force of an accusation. Here is the expanded version, which was uttered just after the agent had paid the claim and which occurred in the presence of others:

15   How did you set the fire? If you rebuild, don't call us. You'll be lucky to find anybody to insure you.

>   *Hunt v. Gerlemann,* 581 S.W.2d 913 (Mo. Ct. App. 1979)

The main illocutionary act to distinguish from accusations is assertions, that is, statements that are (or purport to be) true with no presupposition of badness. Below are the presumed felicity conditions for assertions (first provided in Chapter 3), which you can compare with those for accusing in (14) above.

16   Felicity conditions for asserting:

Semantic content :	Some proposition (i.e., something either true or false)
Preparatory condition:	Speaker believes that Addressee does not believe the proposition. (Note: not "disbelieves…," just "does not believe….")
Sincerity condition:	Speaker believes the proposition.
Essence:	(i) Counts as effort to add the proposition to the common ground;
	(ii) Counts as commitment to the truth of the proposition.

Besides the lack of a presupposition of badness, assertions also are issued with a different perlocutionary aim from accusations. The perlocutionary purpose of an accusation made to an addressee about some other person is to get the addressee to blame the other person for the act or characteristic in question. The perlocutionary purpose of an assertion is just to get addressees to accept that the assertion is true.

Many utterances are ambiguous between being accusations and being just assertions. Tiersma suggests the following factors to distinguish them:

- Use of words like "allegedly," "reportedly," "according to so-and-so," and the like, to signal an assertion;
- One-sidedness vs. even-handedness or balance of presentation;
- Indignation, signaling an accusation; and of course
- Context, including in particular the identity of, and relation between, the speaker and the audience or addressees. Is the utterance made to family members, or to police officers? To colleagues or to superiors?

None of these factors is conclusive. A speaker could pretend to mask what is really an accusation with "allegedly." Example: "Prof. Head threw an eraser at a student...allegedly." The word *allegedly* is uttered after a pause and maybe with a marked intonation. And superficial balance – seemingly presenting just the facts – can be fake. Here's an example from Tiersma showing that what is *not* included can matter:

17   [A] newspaper reported that one woman went to another woman's house and shot her own husband and the other woman. The injured woman sued the newspaper for defamation. The newspaper countered that the report was true. But the report omitted the crucial facts that the plaintiff's husband and others were at the house for a social gathering, and that the perpetrator was angry at her husband for unrelated reasons and only by accident injured the plaintiff. The court held that the facts as reported could be understood as an implicit accusation of infidelity and therefore as defamatory.

Tiersma 1987, 335–336

The traditional approach represented in the definition (12) also suffers from unclarity with respect to *who* the "speaker" is. In the case of your slander of Johnny, it's easy: you. When a newspaper publishes a news story which attributes something bad to someone, the speaker may be the reporter, that is, the actual original "utterer," or, more likely, the newspaper, the employer, who is responsible for employees' acts carried out within the scope of their employment. If the story contains reputation-damaging falsehoods, the reporter and/or the paper could be liable. But not when a news story reports accusations by others. A privilege of **neutral reportage** protects them. Example: in 1972 the New York Times published a news article headlined "Pesticide Spokesmen Accused of 'Lying' on Higher Bird Count." The article was about a fight the Audubon Society was having with pesticide companies. The pesticide companies had pointed to higher bird counts as evidence that their pesticides were not harming bird populations. The Audubon Society argued that the higher bird counts resulted instead from greater numbers of bird watchers with more sophisticated bird-watching practices and greater access to good places for observing birds. The Times reporter interviewed individuals from the Audubon Society and individuals associated with pesticide companies, and quoted one of the former as saying that any scientist who took the pesticide companies' side of the argument was either "someone who is being paid to lie, or is parroting something he knows little about." When the pesticide companies sued, the trial court found the Times liable, but on appeal the Second Circuit held that the Times was not liable, on the grounds of the neutral reportage principle. (*Edwards v. National Audubon Society*, 556 F.2d 113 (2d Cir., 1977))

Look at the definition in (12) again. Taking its word "publication" broadly, as is common in law discourse, notice that some entirely innocent actors might – ridiculously – fall within the scope of the definition: libraries, newsstand owners, even paper deliverers. These entities and individuals can't be expected even to know the content of stories in the items they sell or loan out. The needed fix distinguishes these as **secondary publishers**, who can't be held liable for defamation unless they know the defamatory content and intend to communicate it. Tiersma imagines a way this could occur: "If a patron at the library asked for information about a famous Mr. Jones, the librarian might purposely give him, out of many books, one that she knew falsely accused Mr. Jones of serious offenses. In that case, her act of lending the book shows an intent to communicate and she might conceivably be liable for implicitly accusing Mr. Jones." (Tiersma, *op. cit.*)

What about advertisements? Newspapers are a channel for the ads, that's all; any false and damaging claim in an ad should be the responsibility of the company or person that paid the newspaper to print it. This probably sounds fair, but it isn't how the law has always treated advertisements. In 1960 the New York Times published an advertisement paid for by an advertising company acting for a civil rights group called the Committee to Defend Martin Luther King and the Struggle for Freedom in the South. The ad, headed "Hear Their Rising Voices," was an appeal for money to support the student civil rights movement in the south and for the legal defense of Dr. Martin Luther King Jr. against a perjury charge. Among the many statements in the ad were a few that were false (including some trivial ones like what patriotic song civil rights demonstrators had sung – the national anthem, not "My Country 'Tis of Thee") and some which were vague in ways which implied that the Montgomery, AL, commissioner of public affairs, who was in charge of the police department, was responsible for certain events. This commissioner, L.B. Sullivan, sued the Times for libel, for falsely implying Sullivan's responsibility for "padlocking" the student cafeteria at Alabama State College, a padlocking that had not happened, for "ringing" the campus with police, also untrue, although on three occasions police were deployed near the campus in large numbers, and for a few other events, falsely attributed by implication to Commissioner Sullivan. Writing about this case, Tiersma (1987, *op. cit.*) opined "[I]t stretches credulity to suggest that the New York Times, by accepting a paid advertisement, accused the commissioner..." Nonetheless, Sullivan won at trial and on appeal. However, this result was overturned by the Supreme Court.

Despite the strangeness of a newspaper being sued for defaming someone by printing a paid advertisement, this is not what the case is known for. Rather, the decision was a significant refinement of First Amendment law. In part the Amendment reads "Congress shall make no law...abridging the freedom of speech, or of the press..." But these freedoms are not absolute. You can't lie in court about a material matter, as we saw in the Perjury section; you can't solicit a crime, as we'll see in the next section; and you can't defame someone. The decision distinguished how defamation law was to be applied to public figures as opposed to non-famous private citizens, with a much higher bar required for defamation to be found about public figures. The Court held that

18   [T]he First Amendment protects the publication of all statements, even false ones, about the conduct of public officials except when statements are made with actual malice (with knowledge that they are false or in reckless disregard of their truth or falsity).

New York Times v. Sullivan, 376 U.S. 254 (1964)

This holding needs a little explaining. **Malice** doesn't have its ordinary meaning, but, instead, what's in the parentheses. **Recklessness** isn't defined in the holding. In law it means not caring about likely bad consequences despite being aware of them. It's worse than **negligence**, which means not being as careful as a reasonable person would be in the same circumstances. So you can be found liable for defaming a public figure only if you know that what you publish about that person is false or you were reckless about it. When the Times received the advertisement, it was accompanied by a letter from A. Philip Randolph, a prominent civil rights leader, averring that the signatories whose names appeared at the bottom of the ad had given their permission for the use of their names. This list included leading figures in the arts, religion, and labor unions. At trial the Times' manager of its advertising department testified that he accepted the ad because it was endorsed by lots of individuals of high repute and he had no reason to doubt the veracity of anything in the ad. *New York Times v. Sullivan* has major Constitutional significance but no linguistic significance except insofar as it construes the First Amendment in a way well beyond what the Amendment says, a phenomenon that we'll address in Chapter 8.

5.3 Solicitation

In 1978, the American Nazi Party scheduled a demonstration and march in Skokie, IL, a Chicago suburb where lots of Jews lived. The march was planned for April 20. On March 16, Irving Rubin, a leader of the Jewish Defense League, held a press conference in Los Angeles. He announced plans for a counter-demonstration against the Nazis, and also said the following, holding up five $100 bills:

19   We are offering five hundred dollars, that I have in my hand, to any member of the community, be he Gentile or Jewish, who kills, maims, or seriously injures a member of the American Nazi Party. This offer is being made on the East Coast, on the West Coast. And if they bring us the ears, we'll make it a thousand dollars. The fact of the matter is, that we're deadly serious. This is not said in jest, we are deadly serious.

People v. Rubin, 96 Cal. App. 3d 968 (1979)

Based just on your understanding of the word *solicit,* did Rubin solicit a crime? Here's how criminal solicitation is defined in California law, which we'll use here both because it's typical and because it's the law under which Rubin was prosecuted:

20   Solicitation consists of the asking of another to commit one of the specified crimes with intent that the crime be committed.

People v. Gordon (1975) 47 Cal. App. 3d 465, 472, quoted in *People v. Rubin*

Notice that the cite for the law is a case, not a statute. This is probably because while there is a relevant statute, it isn't a definition:

21   Every person who, with the intent that the crime be committed, solicits another to commit...murder shall be punished by imprisonment in the state prison for three, six, or nine years.

CA Penal Code § 653f(b)

Interestingly, both the definition in *People v. Gordon* and the statute add "intent" to "solicitation," reflecting the semantic intuition that people can insincerely solicit. The Model Penal Code is similar:

22   A person is guilty of solicitation to commit a crime if with the purpose of promoting or facilitating its commission he commands, encourages or requests another person to engage in specific conduct which would constitute such crime or an attempt to commit such crime ...

Model Penal Code § 5.02(1)

The Model Penal Code (MPC) is an influential publication of the American Law Institute that makes recommendations about what the content of most criminal laws should be in U.S. jurisdictions (mainly states, because most criminal laws are state laws). Many states have accepted them in large part, thereby standardizing much state criminal law.

Soliciting is a **Directive**, in Searle's taxonomy (introduced in Chapter 2), along with ordering, requesting, and begging – all of which have the aim of getting one's addressee to do something. Can you ask someone to do something without really wanting them to? Sure. Imagine your boss telling you to have your secretary bring him a cup of coffee. If you don't approve of treating secretaries like restaurant servers, but you're afraid of your boss, you might fulfill your boss's request, privately hoping your secretary (a gutsy person, perhaps) will decline the request as inappropriate. But does this matter? Isn't an insincere request still a request? In the case of solicitation of a crime, isn't the (in)sincerity of the solicitor irrelevant? Apparently not, at least according to the Model Penal Code and in California (and many other states, though not all).

Let's take *requesting* as a typical Directive. The felicity conditions for requesting are presumably those given below (essentially identical to their formulation in Chapter 2 (ex. (2) there)):

23   Felicity conditions for requesting

Semantic content :	Future act A by addressee
Preparatory conditions:	(i) Speaker believes addressee can do A (ii) Speaker assumes that addressee would not do A in the normal course of events
Essence:	Counts as non-enforceable attempt to get addressee to do A

On the assumption that insincere requests are possible, there's no sincerity condition. Criminal solicitation differs from requesting in the criminality of the future act and in the requirement of a sincerity condition:

24   Felicity conditions for criminal solicitation

Semantic content:	Future criminal act A by addressee
Preparatory conditions:	(i) Speaker believes addressee can do A (ii) Speaker assumes that addressee would not do A in the normal course of events
Sincerity condition:	Speaker wants addressee to do A
Essence:	Counts as non-enforceable attempt to get addressee to do A

But hold on. These felicity conditions, both for requests and solicitations, include *addressees*. This is semantically right, because *request* and *solicit* both require the presence of additional expressions – in fact two of them – representing the person requested or solicited and the deed sought. The word sequences

He requested and *She solicited* are ungrammatical because they lack those additional expressions. (The two verbs differ syntactically in what kinds of additional expressions must be overt: with *request* a direct object, as in *He requested a favor*, with *solicit* either a direct or an indirect object, as in *She solicited a loan* and *She solicited an undercover officer.*)

The question is whether the indirect object has to refer to a specific individual. If Irving Rubin had said to the author of this book "I am offering $500 to you, Jeff Kaplan, to kill, maim, or seriously injure a member of the American Nazi Party," there would be little question that Rubin had solicited a crime. (Some jurisdictions require, for conviction for solicitation, proof that the recipient of the solicitation did receive it – so Rubin might get off if Jeff Kaplan was unaware of the solicitation.) In the actual case, Rubin's solicitation – if it really was one – was directed at anybody and everybody.

The alternative is that it wasn't a genuine solicitation, but political hyperbole, protected by the First Amendment. Here's an example of the latter: In 1964, a Ku Klux Klan representative named Clarence Brandenburg invited members of the Cincinnati, Ohio, press to a KKK rally at a farm. They filmed what happened there. A small number of men burned a cross and made some speeches, saying, for example, "[I]f our President, our Congress, our Supreme Court, continues to suppress the white, Caucasian race, it's possible that there might have to be some revengeance (*sic*) taken," "This what we're going to do to the niggers," and "Personally, I believe the nigger should be returned to Africa, the Jew returned to Israel." Brandenburg was found guilty for violating an Ohio law which prohibited

[25]   advocat[ing] ... the duty, necessity, or propriety of crime, sabotage, violence, or unlawful methods of terrorism as a means of accomplishing industrial or political reform

Ohio Rev.Code Ann. § 2923.13

Brandenburg's appeal resulted in a landmark 1969 Supreme Court decision protecting free speech. Reversing Brandenburg's conviction, the Court unanimously held

26   [T]he constitutional guarantees of free speech and free press
     do not permit a State to forbid or proscribe advocacy of the
     use of force or of law violation except where such advocacy is
     directed to inciting or producing imminent lawless action and
     is likely to incite or produce such action.

                              Brandenburg v. Ohio, 395 U.S. 444 (1969)

The Court thus created a three-part test to distinguish advocacy
(protected) from criminal solicitation (unlawful): whether the
speech was *aimed at* "producing *imminent* lawless action" and
whether the speech was *likely* to produce such lawless action.

Back to Irving Rubin and his $500 offer. How do you think Rubin
should have fared under this three-part test? The fact that Rubin
uttered his words during a press conference is evidence that it was
political theater intended to get publicity from media attention; if
Rubin had the aim only of actually soliciting a murder, rather than
intending to make a public political point, he could have made his
offer in a more private context. Ordinary solicitations of murder
occur this way. Someone who wants to have someone bumped off
usually seeks to hire an assassin very circumspectly, not out in the
public eye the way Rubin did, at a press conference he called himself. What's more, ordinary solicitors of bad acts solicit them typically in allusive language rather than explicitly the way Rubin did.
So whatever else it did, Rubin's utterance was an effort to make a
political point. If that's all it did, under *Brandenburg* it was entitled
to First Amendment protection. The question is what else it did.

Was Rubin's *actual purpose* to solicit murder? If so, would the
murder be "*imminent?*" And were Rubin's words *likely* to lead to
murder? The first question is about Rubin's mental state, which
cannot be observed directly. The second question requires a
judgment about how "imminent" an act of the sort in question a
month away would be (assuming that Rubin's utterance was about
a murder that would take place at the Skokie march). The third
question requires a conclusion about how probable it was that the
act in question would actually come off.

Evidence for actual purpose comes from Rubin's explicit averral
of it: "…we're deadly serious. This is not said in jest, we are deadly

serious." On the other hand, doubling the payoff for bringing the victim's ears makes the "offer" sound less serious. As noted by the appellate court, imminence is relative. An act planned to occur at a demonstration five weeks away can be compared with other public events similarly scheduled. The court wrote "[A] Papal visit to Belfast, a Soviet chief of state's visit to Rome, a presidential campaign trip to Dallas, and a presidential inauguration in Washington, can each be said to be proximate and imminent, even though occurrence may be some weeks away." Your intuitions may vary. As for likelihood, the court opined that the probability of murder actually occurring might have been higher if Rubin had named a specific American Nazi Party member as the target.

The court in *Rubin* did not have to resolve any of these questions. The appeal – by the prosecution – had been from the trial court's decision to set aside Rubin's indictment. There is a high bar to overturn an indictment, since all that's needed for an indictment is a reasonable suspicion that the suspect had committed a crime. So what the appellate court decided was that there was enough reason to believe that Rubin's words were criminal for a court to need to give this question a full examination at a trial. Rubin stood trial and ... (drum roll) ... was acquitted.

By way of summary, the legal view toward the illocutionary act of soliciting a crime includes as a necessary element the speaker's sincerity: the speaker has to be serious, not just engaging in hyperbole. In addition, for an illocutionary solicitation to rise to the level of a crime, the prospective crime must be both *imminent* and *likely.* If you are so angry at Johnny that you offer your large violence-disposed buddy Bruno $50 to beat Johnny up tonight, you're probably guilty of criminal solicitation. But if the proposed beating is for when Johnny graduates three years from now, even if that's somehow likely, it's not imminent, and you'll probably get off.

There's one final issue. What if the beating is for tonight but unknown to you Bruno is actually not inclined to violence at all – he's really a gentle soul who wouldn't hurt a flea? Based on the large number of convictions for solicitations of undercover police officers to carry out criminal acts, what matters is not actual likelihood, but the soliciting individual's *belief* that it's likely. If law enforcement gets wind of your proposal to Bruno, you're probably in trouble even if Bruno, unknown to you, is a pacifist.

5.4 Conspiracy

Again we'll use a true story. Warning: it's about a horrible plan. The good news is that it didn't come off. A Minnesota man named Marlin Olson wanted his mother dead. He proposed a deal to his cousin, Robert Zobel: For $125,000, to be paid over a period of years, Zobel would go to Mrs. Olson's house when Olson's father was away, gain admission – Mrs. Olson was his aunt – and break her neck, put her body in the trunk of his car, drive to a river, weight the body with bricks, and dump it in the river. Zobel discussed the plan with Olson, but a day or so later told the police about it. He may have initially been interested, who knows, but he testified at Olson's trial that he never intended to take part in the plan. The police told him to play along. On the day scheduled for the murder, Olson and Zobel learned that Dad Olson might not be away after all, occasioning a change in plans. Now Olson would call his father and tell him he had car trouble and ask him to come and help, and then call Zobel to tell him the coast was clear and he should go ahead with the plan. On the appointed day all this happened, with the police aware of what was happening at every step. The last phone call, the one from Olson to Zobel to give him the go-ahead, was taped, and soon after that phone call ended, Olson was arrested.

Olson was charged with conspiracy to commit murder. Here's the relevant Minnesota statute:

27 Whoever conspires with another to commit a crime and in furtherance of the conspiracy one or more of the parties does some overt act in furtherance of such conspiracy may be sentenced as follows...

Minn. St. 609.175 Subd. 2

Olson was convicted. He was also convicted of attempted murder. He appealed.

The "overt act" requirement in the statute in (27) is common (though not universal) in conspiracy statutes. That's not what's interesting about this statute. What's interesting is the first part, "Whoever conspires with another." Contrast an earlier version of this statute:

28   When two or more persons shall conspire:
   (1) To commit a crime;
   ...
   "Every such person shall be guilty...

Minn. St.1961, § 613.70

The version in (28) is about two or more people conspiring, the version in (27) about *one* person "conspiring with another." In law talk (27) is called **unilateral** and (28) is called **bilateral.** The semantic question is whether it is possible for one person to conspire with another without the second person conspiring. It's also the legal question, one about which there is controversy.

A leading reason offered for the older, bilateral, approach was about the nature of "agreeing," an argument semantic in nature:

29   Conspiracy is the agreement of two or more to effect an unlawful purpose. Two people cannot agree unless they both intend to carry out the purpose which is stated to be the object of their combination. Therefore there is no agreement, and consequently no conspiracy, where one of the two never intends to carry out the unlawful purpose.

Fridman, Mens Rea in Conspiracy,
19 Modern L.Rev. 276 (1956)

The author of the article cited above, G.H.L. Fridman, disagreed with this approach. He favored instead the unilateral approach:

30   "The fact that, unknown to a man who wishes to enter a con-spiracy to commit some criminal purpose, the other person has no intention of fulfilling that purpose ought to be irrele-vant as long as the first man does intend to fulfill it if he can"

because "a man who believes he is conspiring to commit a crime and wishes to conspire to commit a crime has a guilty mind and has done all in his power to plot the commission of an unlawful purpose."

Id.

This argument is not linguistic, but psychological and normative, in concluding that the law "should" treat as guilty a would-be conspirator who tries to plan a crime with a secretly fake conspirator, because of the person's "guilty mind" and the person's action to "plot" a crime.

Since we're doing law and linguistics, let's look more closely at the semantics of *conspire*. The verb *conspire* is a **reciprocal** verb, like *meet, marry, correspond, fight, rhyme,* and *hug*. The defining property of reciprocal verbs is the entailment relation shown in the examples in (31). (A sentence S_1 **entails** a sentence S_2 when if S_1 is true then necessarily so is S_2.)

31	Sarah and Lee hugged	*entails*	Sarah hugged Lee Lee hugged Sarah
	Sarah and Lee corresponded	*entails*	Sarah corresponded with Lee Lee corresponded with Sarah
	Sarah and Lee conspired to rig the election	*entails*	Sarah conspired with Lee to rig the election Lee conspired with Sarah to rig the election

Call the structure on the left the **conjoined subject structure**, and the structure on the right the **separated structure**.

Strong reciprocal verbs, like *marry,* entail in the other direction too, from the separated structure to the conjoined subject structure:

32	Sarah married Lee	*entails both*	Sarah and Lee (got) married *and* Lee and Sarah (got) married

Weak reciprocals, like *hug,* don't:

33	Sarah hugged Lee	*does not entail either*	Sarah and Lee hugged *or* Lee and Sarah hugged

With strong reciprocal verbs, both versions of the separated structure entail each other. Not so with weak ones:

34   Strong: Sarah married Lee <==> Lee married Sarah
           Weak: Sarah hugged Lee <=/ => Lee hugged Sarah

(The double-pointed arrow means that the entailment goes in both directions. The double-pointed arrow with the slash means that neither sentence entails the other.)

Another test to distinguish strong from weak reciprocal verbs is whether negating a separated sentence results in contradiction: yes in the case of strong reciprocals, no in the case of weak ones:

35   #Sarah married Lee, but Lee didn't marry Sarah. *Contradictory.*

    #The first word rhymes with the fourth word, but the fourth word doesn't rhyme with the first word. *Contradictory.*

    Sarah hugged Lee, but Lee didn't hug Sarah. *Not contradictory.*

What about *conspire*? Is it a strong, or a weak, reciprocal verb? If it's weak, Olson's defense argument is weak too; it's possible for one person to conspire with another without them both conspiring. Guilty!

If it's strong, his defense argument has linguistic support; one person conspiring with another necessarily has the second conspiring with the first.

So, here we go. Check your intuitions: Does *Sarah conspired with Lee to rig the election* entail *Sarah and Lee conspired to rig the election*? Does *Sarah conspired with Lee* entail *Lee conspired with Sarah*? Is it contradictory to say *Sarah conspired with Lee but Lee didn't conspire with Sarah*?

Intuitions about these may vary. You might try to sharpen your intuitions by looking at other reciprocal verbs (*meet, fight, date, argue,* and *correspond* may be useful ones).

Here's the holding from the appellate court's opinion:

36   [T]he Minnesota statute as it presently reads [*(27), the later version*] ... is now phrased in unilateral terms ["*whoever conspires with another"*]...

Because of this wording, we hold that the trial court was free to convict defendant of conspiracy under the facts of this case.

State v. St. Christopher, 232 N.W.2d 798 (1975)

(The name "St. Christopher" is there because Olson legally changed his name.)

Olson was planning to accomplish a very bad thing, and he *did* a very bad thing, trying to arrange the murder of his own mother. Just looking at moral considerations of crime, punishment, and justice, he shouldn't have gotten off, and he didn't. But looking at the meaning of the statute, rather than justice, did the appeals court get it right in deciding that "because of this wording" – the structure of the statute with the separated NPs – Olson's conviction should be upheld?

The court in the case argued for its interpretation more fully than simply pointing to "this wording." To justify its holding the court also cited the Model Penal Code's definition of conspiracy, a unilateral one, and accompanying commentary.

37   Model Penal Code's definition of conspiracy:

A person is guilty of conspiracy with another person or persons to commit a crime if with the purpose of promoting or facilitating its commission he:

(a) agrees with such other person or persons that they or one or more of them will engage in conduct which constitutes such crime or an attempt or solicitation to commit such crime...

Model Penal Code sec. 5.03(1)

38   Model Penal Code's commentary on its definition of conspiracy

> [In cases] where the person with whom the defendant conspired secretly intends not to go through with the plan..., the culpable party's guilt would not be affected by the fact that the other party's agreement was feigned. He has conspired, within the meaning of the definition, in the belief that the other party was with him; apart from the issue of entrapment often presented in such cases, his culpability is not decreased by the other's secret intention.

Because of the true plotter's belief about the other party and the criminal intention of the true plotter, the true plotter can't escape guilt for conspiracy. Interestingly, the commentary observes in a part not quoted above that the vote on the recommendation for the unilateral approach was only 14–11, the minority voters seeing the unilateral approach as vitiating the point of conspiracy laws, namely, to proscribe criminal *group* activity.

The court did not engage in semantic analysis. Besides stating that its decision comported with the words of the statute, it justified the unilateral approach in terms of justice, specifically how unjust it would be to let off someone who planned a crime with another believing mistakenly that the other person was planning to participate. Rather than looking closely at the semantics of *conspire,* the court fitted its justice-motivated desired outcome into the purview of the statute, because the wording of the statute *permitted* that outcome.

At this point you have presumably concluded that the court got it right, got it wrong, or you're not sure. Next you should be asking yourself what *should* be the effect of semantics (including semantic variability in intuitions) on law. For example, what *should* happen if a judge learns that the words in a statute mean, to the speech community, something different from what he or she thinks they mean? Or that there's a divide among native speakers on the meaning of words in a statute? Should the judge just rely on his or her semantic intuitions? One possible value of courts' accepting semantic findings is that they have the potential to correct (possibly unconscious) judicial "backwards" reasoning – reasoning from a desired result back to arguments justifying it. Attorneys representing clients develop arguments this way all the time; in fact, they are professionally required to. Judges are emphatically not supposed to.

Issues such as these are a big part of the analysis of statutory interpretation, which we'll take up in Chapter 8.

5.5 Conclusion

In this chapter we've looked at perjury, defamation, solicitation, and conspiracy. Regarding perjury, using a Gricean lens to understand it led to a suggestion for a sharper definition of perjury that recognizes the difference between manifest violations of Relevance and covert ones.

Regarding defamation, following Tiersma's suggestion of defining it as "public accusation" permitted a speech act account. Accusations differ from assertions in having a presupposition of badness of an act by, or characteristic of, a person. Because accusations are speech acts, they have speakers, raising the real-world issue of who a speaker is, for example a reporter or the newspaper they work for. Defamation also raises First Amendment issues, addressed importantly in *New York Times v. Sullivan,* a Supreme Court decision with great significance for freedom of speech and of the press.

Our look at solicitation led to a distinction between the speech acts of requesting and criminal solicitation, the latter but not the former requiring speaker sincerity. Solicitation raises freedom of speech issues, addressed by *Brandenburg v. Ohio:* criminal behavior can be advocated but not solicited, the difference hinging on the speaker's intent, the imminence of the potential behavior, and the likelihood of the behavior actually taking place.

Finally, our discussion of conspiracy required a visit to the semantics of reciprocal verbs, to add linguistic depth to the legal world's distinction between unilateral and bilateral approaches to conspiracy. This discussion also forced us to raise the question of the relevance to statutory interpretation of linguistic findings about meaning, foreshadowing a deeper look at this question in Chapter 8.

Additional readings of interest

Space limitations prevent inclusion of a section on threats. If you are interested in a linguistic analysis of threatening, read the paper and case referenced below.

Kaplan, Jeffrey P. 2016. Case report: *Elonis v. United States.* International Journal of Speech, Language, and the Law 23 (2): 275–92.

Elonis v. United States, 575 U.S. (2015).

Chapter 6

The "language" of the law

6.0 Introduction

Let's say you're a college senior getting ready to apply to law school. In a newsletter for lawyers, in an article about a couple of colorful lawyers, you encounter the following sentence:

1   Referring to the action he had brought over the integration clause, after he filed his amended complaint adding the allegation about the liquidated damages provision, Burr said he had not expected Hamilton's demurrer to reference the parol evidence rule.

You know, or can guess, that an "action" is a lawsuit, and that a "complaint" that one can "file" must be a formal statement specifying what a defendant has allegedly done to damage someone, but you're lost when it comes to the "liquidated damages provision," a "demurrer," and the "parol evidence rule." Jargon like this suggests to you that part of becoming a lawyer must require learning the "language" of the law.

Reading on, you learn that the story is about conflicting interpretations of a contract. You read the following quote from a letter from the complaining party:

2   Please be advised that the goods furnished by you to me on or about 9/28/2018 under our contract entered into by and between

us on 5/27/2018 are defective in the following respects: ...; and I intend to assert all my legal rights pertaining thereto.

This isn't so bad. Formal and legal-sounding, yes, but entirely understandable.

Look again at (1). If you replace the jargon with familiar words, notice what happens:

3   Referring to the action he had brought over the bread clause, after he filed his amended complaint adding the allegation about the spoiled yeast provision, Burr said he had not expected Hamilton's response to reference the peanut butter rule.

You can almost understand it. The point is that incomprehensibility to laypeople of the "language" of the law is a matter of words, not syntactic structure. With a few exceptions, the syntax of legal English is the syntax of English.

6.1 Historical reasons for "legal English"

Because of the United States' origin as a British colony, American law, and its "language," is a direct descendant of English law and its language. English, and American, legal discourse uses lots of words and phrases unique to it like *liquidated damages, demurrer,* and *parol evidence;* lots of familiar English words with special meanings in law like *action,* a fair amount of Latin expressions, like *amicus curiae,* and a similar dosage of French, such as *en banc* and *voir dire.*

Before we go on, it's only fair to tell you what these pieces of jargon mean:

4   *Liquidated damages:* **Damages** are money amounts a **plaintiff** (complaining party) can be awarded as a result of a winning lawsuit. **Liquidated** damages are amounts pre-set in a contract in case one party breaches the contract.
Demurrer: a formal response to a complaint filed in a lawsuit.
Parol evidence rule: In contract disputes, this rule prohibits evidence about oral agreements alleged to have been made

which differ from a contract's written terms; this rule restricts a contract's terms to those written in the contract. Note: In most jurisdictions, there are exceptions to the rule. For example, if a contract is ambiguous, parol evidence may be admitted to resolve the ambiguity.

Amicus curiae: "friend of the court," describing written arguments – **briefs** – submitted to a court by third parties.

En banc: "in/on (the) bench," describing a multi-judge appeals court with all member judges deciding a case together.

Voir dire: "truly to say," the process of questioning prospective jurors to determine their qualifications for jury service in a case. (Note: The French word *voir* here is from Latin *verum,* "truth," not modern French *voir* "to see.")

The presence of Latin and French expressions in our legal discourses is due to two factors. First, accidents of history: In the middle ages in England, Latin was the language of literacy. Even after the imposition of French as the language of the ruling class after the Norman conquest in 1066, statutes were written in Latin, a pattern that continued until around 1300, after which French largely, but not completely, supplanted Latin. French continued as the primary language of English law until around 1600, even though it had been replaced by English as the primary spoken language even of the ruling class (Tiersma 2012).

The second factor – really two similar factors – is conservatism, in writing and in law. The relative permanence of written documents limits change in written language; hence "unphonetic" spellings persist like the "gh" in *fight, thought, and rough* and the "k" in *knight* and *knife* – written vestiges of earlier pronunciations. In law, written records of courts' decisions and written statutes also helps preserve old forms of legal expressions.

And law itself is conservative too, for consistency and reliability over time, as can be seen, for example, in the importance of **precedent**, courts' reliance on earlier court decisions. Legal conservatism extends even to present day courts' unwillingness to change previously used jury instructions, lest changes introduce unforeseen consequences leading to reversal on appeal.

Then there is **borrowing**, an inaccurate term for one language taking in words from another. The Norman conquest resulted in a vast number of French words coming into English, with an even greater proportional effect in legal discourses, because the French-speaking ruling class after the Norman conquest was the creator and executor of law. Borrowing of French into English legal discourse has even resulted in at least one grammatical pattern foreign to English: in certain frozen expressions, adjectives occurring after, rather than before, the nouns they modify. Examples: *attorney general, malice aforethought, court martial.*

6.2 Syntactic and semantic characteristics of legal discourses

The generalization above that the syntax of legal English is the syntax of English was hedged: "with a few exceptions." Below we'll describe some exceptions.

6.2.1 Co-reference patterns

One area of difference between ordinary English and legal English has to do with later occurrences of co-referring expressions. The technical linguistic term is **anaphor(ic)**; an anaphor is a pronoun or other expression that gets its reference from another expression in the same discourse. The general English rule is to use pronouns for later occurrences: *[My friend Jane] came for my birthday. [She] took me to four different bars.* But often in law discourses, pronouns are avoided and full noun phrases occur instead: *[Seller] promises that [seller] will...* This pronoun-avoidance syntactic pattern correlates with a difference in semantic interpretation. In English generally, repeated identical names are ordinarily interpreted with different referents. *Jane gave me Jane's book* is probably about two different Janes. Not so in law English.

6.2.1.1 Here- and there- plus prepositions

Another pattern involving co-reference (or **anaphora**) is the use of *here* and *there* with prepositional suffixes: *herein, thereof,* and the like. In these words, the *here* or *there* part is like a pronoun, getting its reference from context. Example:

5   Such petition shall be under oath, sworn to by the petitioner or, if the petitioner if a corporation, by a duly authorized officer or agent *thereof...*

Fla. Stat. § 812.061 (1)

In this example, *thereof* can be paraphrased *of it*. The **antecedent** (an expression elsewhere in the same discourse providing the referent for a pronoun) of the *there* part of *thereof* in (5) is *a corporation*. This pronoun use of *there* is insensitive to number. In (5) it's singular, because *a corporation* is singular. In the following example it's plural

6   United States deeds and patents and copies *thereof...*

Fla. Stat. § 92.14

with the paraphrase *of them* and the antecedent *United States deeds and patents.*

Most pronouns can get their reference either from linguistic context, that is, antecedents, as in the above examples, or from context-of-utterance, as in *There he goes!,* uttered by a baseball fan who sees a baserunner take off to attempt to steal a base. In that example, there's no antecedent for *he;* rather, listeners get its reference from the runner himself in the extra-linguistic context. Such uses are called **deictic**, from the Greek word for "to point." Words with *here,* like *herein* and *hereto,* in legal language are deictic, referring to the discourse in which they occur, with paraphrases like *in this* and *to this,* as in this one:

7   This License Agreement, including the exhibits attached *hereto* and...incorporated by this reference (together, the "Agreement"), is entered into effective as of the date shown in the Sales Quote...

https://vs-corp.com/wp-content/uploads/2018/02/VS-License AgreementExhibitA-1.pdf

In (7), the *here* part of *hereto* refers to the document.

The following example helpfully lists a bunch of *here+preposition* words and defines them as having a particular deictic reference –

8   Hereby, herein, hereinabove, hereinafter, hereinbefore, hereof, hereto and hereunder refer to this Consolidated Local Improvements Law and not solely to the particular portion thereof in which such word is used.

NV Rev Stat § 271.120 (2013)

– namely, the (whole) Consolidated Local Improvements Law. These words occur outside legal discourses –

9   Can you find anything in these three theories or combinations *thereof* that can account for the decline of the Methodists and the increase of the Baptists?

Greeley, Andrew M. Sociology and Religion: A Collection of Readings (1995), www.collinsdictionary.com/us/dictionary/english/thereof

– thereby (ha!) providing a bit of evidence that "the language of the law" is a misnomer.

6.2.1.2 Said

Also in the area of anaphora is the use of *said,* as in the following example:

10   Whereas, the San Jose Country Club is an association of individuals organized together for social and athletic purposes, pursuant to the constitution and by-laws heretofore adopted by *said* association; And whereas, this is a regularly called and held meeting of the council of the *said* San Jose Country Club...

www.sanjosecountryclub.org/files/1912%20Resolution%20to%20Purchase%20SJ%20Golf%20_%20Country%20Club.pdf

Said can be used as a determiner, as in its first occurrence above, and as an adjective (or past participle), as in the second. As a determiner, *said* can typically be paraphrased by *the* or by demonstratives (*this, these*), and as an adjective by *aforementioned*. Given its obvious morphological nature – past participle of the verb *say* – it's not surprising that *said* can be used only with antecedents; unlike *the* or demonstratives, it can't occur in noun phrases used to refer to extralinguistic referents:

11   a. Wow. The / that moon is amazing tonight.
      b. *Wow. Said moon is amazing tonight.

Such (determiner and adjective) uses of *said* are not restricted to legal discourses, although non-law uses can feel jokey, the humor coming from the contrast between the formal *said* and informal content in the context:

12   a. There was silly putty, coloring books and crayons, invisible ink books, a slinky, and other little odds and ends. When she would get antsy it was fun for her to rifle through and pick something new to do! It's ironic though that my water broke while standing in line at Michael's to pay for *said* items.

      www.mommyinsports.com/2015/08/things-to-do-with-your-toddler-while-feeding-baby-2.html, cited in Stevers 2017

      b. Ya know we have these wonderful joyous events called "Baby Showers". These are fantastic and fun events where the parents are gifted with many adorable items for their soon to be born little adorable terrors… oops I mean babies!;) We as the friend's of the *said* parents-to-be get them cute little outfits, stuffed animals and many other fun items. …

      http://blessedtobelogansmommy.blogspot.com/2011/06/carpet-cleaners-should-comewith-each.html. *Id.*

6.2.2 Tendencies, not rules

Some syntactic differences are not rules, but tendencies, such as the common use of extremely long and complex sentences in contracts and statutes. Tiersma 2006 cites a sentence in a contract that is over 1400 words long. Legal English also has lots of passives, especially agentless ones. Example: *All changes shall promptly be disclosed... failure shall be deemed a material breach...* It also has lots of third persons instead of first and second. Example: *Buyer agrees to pay Seller...* instead of *I agree to pay you...* and *The court rules that...*, spoken by a judge, instead of *I rule that...*

6.3 Canons for interpretation

Judges have recourse to a number of principles they can apply to construe statutes and Constitutional provisions, known as **canons**. Some have only legal content, such as the rule that if possible, statutes should be construed to avoid raising Constitutional questions But some are specifically linguistic.

6.3.1 Noscitur a sociis

The Latin translates as "It is known by its neighbors." The idea is that a string of words should, if possible, be understood in a way that treats them all as similar in meaning. For example, if a statute lists "tacks, staples, nails, brads, and screws," the interpretation should treat the meanings of all the listed nouns as fasteners, ruling out interpretations of *staples* as "basic food items" and *nails* as fingernails and toenails (Scalia & Garner 2012: 196). Here's a case example from 1961. The question was how to apply a then-operative section of the Internal Revenue Code which provided tax breaks for "income resulting from exploration, discovery, or prospecting." Two corporations wanted those tax breaks for income they had gained from sales of revolutionary new products in the 1950s, the motion sickness medicine Dramamine and Polaroid 60-second photograph development cameras. Both corporations argued that their innovations resulted from "discoveries," thereby permitting the tax advantages. Invoking *noscitur a sociis,* Chief Justice Earl Warren said No:

[13]   "Discovery" is a word usable in many contexts, and with various shades of meaning. Here, however, it does not stand

alone, but gathers meaning from the words around it. These words strongly suggest that a precise and narrow application was intended in [the statute]. The three words in conjunction, "exploration," "discovery," and "prospecting," all describe income-producing activity in the oil and gas and mining industries, but it is difficult to conceive of any other industry to which they all apply. Certainly the development and manufacturer of drugs and cameras are not such industries. The maxim *noscitur a sociis*, that a word is known by the company it keeps, while not an inescapable rule, is often wisely applied where a word is capable of many meanings in order to avoid the giving of unintended breadth to the Acts of Congress. ... The application of the maxim here leads to the conclusion that "discovery" in [the statute] means only the discovery of mineral resources.

Jarecki v. G. D. Searle & Co., 367 U.S. 303 (1961)

6.3.2 Ejusdem generis

The one is similar to *noscitur a sociis*. The translation is "of the same kind." The idea is that when a general term follows a sequence of expressions, linked to the preceding sequence by *and* or *or,* the general term's denotation is limited to things of the same type as those on the list. For example, a statute mentioning "furniture, clothes, kitchen items, tools, and all other property" should be construed as referring to personal property, not real estate (an example adapted from Scalia & Garner, *id.,* p. 199). Here's a case example: The Federal Arbitration Act (FAA) required that arbitration provisions in employment contracts be enforced, but with an exception: "contracts of employment of seamen, railroad employees, or any other class of workers engaged in foreign or interstate commerce." A salesman at Circuit City Stores named Saint Clair Adams sued Circuit City in a California state court for discrimination having to do with his sexual orientation. His employment contract contained a clause requiring arbitration, instead of lawsuits, of any employment-related disputes between him and Circuit City. Circuit City countersued in federal court seeking enforcement of the arbitration clause in the contract, and won. On appeal to the Ninth Circuit, Adams argued that the exception in the FAA covered him: he was a "worker engaged in...interstate commerce." He was, and he won. Yay! Not so fast. Circuit City appealed to the Supreme Court, where *it* won, 5–4. Justice Kennedy's majority opinion invoked *ejusdem generis* to interpret the exception part of the FAA to include only interstate commerce workers who worked in *transportation.*

14   [T]he words "any other class of workers engaged in ... commerce" constitute a residual phrase, following, in the same sentence, explicit reference to "seamen" and "railroad employees." ...The wording ... calls for the application of the maxim *ejusdem generis*, the statutory canon that "[w]here general words follow specific words in a statutory enumeration, the general words are construed to embrace only objects similar in nature to those objects enumerated by the preceding specific words." (citation omitted) Under this rule of construction the residual clause should be read to give effect to the terms "seamen" and "railroad employees," and should itself be controlled and defined by reference to the enumerated categories of workers which are recited just before it...

Circuit City Stores, Inc., v. Adams, 532 U.S. 105 (2001)

Finding *ejusdem generis* commonalities is not always straightforward. A federal law called the Armed Career Criminal Act (ACCA) defines *violent felony* as (among other things) "any crime punishable by imprisonment for a term exceeding one year...that...is burglary, arson, or extortion, involves the use of explosives, or *otherwise involves conduct that presents a serious potential risk of physical injury to another*" (18 U.S.C. § 924(e)(2)(B)(ii)). The italicized part is another "residual clause." It's pretty vague. Does *attempted* burglary fit? Driving under the influence of alcohol (DUI)? Failure to report to prison? Vehicle flight? **Have a look at the following cases.** The results might surprise you. **Be sure to read the dissents**.

James v. United States, 550 U.S. 192 (2007) (attempted burglary);
Begay v. United States, 553 U.S. 137 (2008) (DUI);
Chambers v. United States, 555 U.S. 122 (2009) (failure to report to prison);
Sykes v. United States, 564 U.S. 1 (2011) (vehicle flight).

Now, if you feel up to it, read *Johnson v. U.S.,* 576 U.S. __, 135 S. Ct. 2551 (2015), a decision finding the residual clause in the ACCA unconstitutional, on due process grounds, because of its vagueness.

6.3.3 Canons for disambiguation

Because the interpretation of legally operative discourses has to be consistent, the judicial system has rules for dealing with unintended ambiguities. Some of these rules are motivated by fairness or public policy concerns, for instance the **rule of lenity**, which requires ambiguous provisions to be construed favorably to criminal defendants. Suppose a guy named Gus is arrested for violating a statute that prohibits "knowingly carrying a firearm without a permit." At trial Gus's defense is that that he "knowingly" carried a firearm but did not know that he needed a permit to do so and that the thought of needing a permit to carry his firearm had never occurred to him. His lawyer points out the ambiguity in the statute: *knowingly* modifies the whole stretch *carries a firearm without a permit,* as in (15a), or just *carries a firearm,* as in (15b):

15   a.   b.

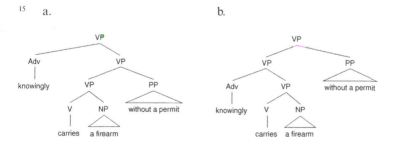

If read with the structure in (15b), Gus would be guilty, because (i) he knew he was carrying a firearm and (ii) he had no permit to do so, regardless of his knowledge. If read with the structure in (15a), the prosecution would have to prove that he knew that his firearm-carrying was permitless. Under the rule of lenity, the statute is taken as having the (a) structure.

Some of these disambiguating rules are not motivated by policy concerns, but just aim for interpretive consistency, by imposing a preference for one reading of a given type of ambiguous structure over another. Example: the **last antecedent** rule, which says that a modifying expression that occurs after what it modifies should be understood as modifying the last possible modify-ee. Consider (16).

16   These regulations shall not apply to kayaks, canoes, or rowboats less than 16 feet long.

In (16), the modifying expression *less than 16 feet long* can be taken as modifying the whole sequence *kayaks, canoes, or rowboats,* or as modifying just *rowboats.* The last antecedent rule mandates the latter interpretation.

Frustratingly, there's a rule that goes exactly the other way, dubbed by some the **series qualifier** canon (Scalia & Garner 2012). Sequences like *great beer and burgers* are syntactically ambiguous as to the scope of the modifier, with the adjective modifying the first possible modify-ee (here, *beer*) or the whole sequence (here, *beer and burgers*). The series qualifier rule imposes a disambiguating principle: a modifying expression applies to a whole sequence of grammatically possible modify-ees. Consider the ambiguous expressions in (17):

17   a. high crimes and misdemeanors
     b. a partnership or corporation registered in Delaware

Under the series qualifier rule, (17a) should be understood as meaning "high crimes and high misdemeanors," and (17b) as meaning "a partnership registered in Delaware or a corporation registered in Delaware."

There seems to be no principled way to tell which of these two canons should apply in a particular case, and it's interesting that Scalia & Garner's discussion of the series qualifier canon immediately follows their discussion of the last antecedent canon, with no comment about the clash between them. This problem may extend beyond the contradiction just identified; in a famous paper, Karl Llewellyn (1950) argues, with examples, that *most* interpretive canons are contradicted by others.

6.3.4 Canons representing Gricean communicative expectations

6.3.4.1 Expressio unius est exclusio alterius

The translation of the Latin is "Expression of one thing is exclusion of another." This canon is a manifestation of Gricean Quantity, the expectation that speakers will provide as much information as is contextually required. Suppose someone tells you "I have three classes this term." By "expressing" their having three classes, they have implied the "exclusion" of having any more. Utterances whose interpretation depend on this expectation can have the "exclusion" cancelled, as in "I have three classes this term, in fact four." The possibility of cancellation exists in legal discourses just as in the wider world:

[18]   (1)   Upon all roadways of sufficient width, a vehicle shall be driven upon the right half of the roadway, except as follows:
(a)   When overtaking and passing another vehicle proceeding in the same direction under the rules governing such movement;...

Fla. Stat. § 316.081. www.leg.state.fl.us/Statutes/index. cfm?App_mode=Display_Statute&URL=0300-0399/0316/ Sections/0316.081.html

In this example, the first clause implicates that vehicles must be driven *only* on the right, an implicature immediately canceled by the "except" clause.

6.3.4.2   The "no surplusage" canon

This canon requires that all words of a statute or Constitutional provision must be given effect. This canon reflects a commonsense expectation about ordinary communication, one given theoretical status in Grice's Maxim of Relevance – in the strong formulation, "Maximize relevance." This canon is ignored in some redundant conjoined-synonym expressions in legal language like *will and testament* and *indemnify and hold harmless*. But otherwise, the "no surplusage" rule can be a useful interpretive tool. Here's an example from a case discussed above, *Circuit City Stores v. Adams*. That case – remember? – was about a statute excepting from an arbitration requirement "contracts of employment of seamen, railroad employees, or any other class of workers engaged in foreign or interstate commerce." The issue was whether a Circuit City salesman, who unquestionably worked in interstate commerce, could escape forced arbitration. Our discussion above quoted Justice Kennedy's majority opinion holding that *ejusdem generis* justified a No answer. In the same part of that opinion Justice Kennedy implicitly invoked the "no surplusage" canon:

[19]   Construing the residual phrase to exclude all employment contracts fails to give independent effect to the statute's enumeration of the specific categories of workers which precedes it; there would be no need for Congress to use the phrases "seamen" and "railroad employees" if those same classes of workers were subsumed within the meaning of the "engaged in … commerce" residual clause.

Circuit City v. Adams, op. cit.

Here's another example. Police pulled a driver named Roland Bailey over because his car lacked a front license plate and an inspection sticker. More trouble came his way when he couldn't produce a driver's license. Searching the car, the cops found 27 bags of cocaine, and, in the trunk, a lot of cash and a loaded pistol. Bailey was arrested, tried, and convicted of several crimes, including violating a federal statute imposing a five-year sentence on anyone who "during and in relation to any crime of violence or drug trafficking crime ... uses or carries a firearm" (18 U. S. C. § 924(c)(1)). Bailey appealed but lost. The appellate court held that the gun in the trunk could have facilitated Bailey's drug dealing, and this could constitute "using" it. The Supreme Court reversed, partly on "surplusage" grounds:

[20] Looking past the word "use" itself, we read § 924(c)(1) with the assumption that Congress intended each of its terms [here, "uses" and "carries"] to have meaning. "Judges should hesitate ... to treat [as surplusage] statutory terms in any setting, and resistance should be heightened when the words describe an element of a criminal offense." (cite omitted) Here, Congress has specified two types of conduct with a firearm: "uses" or "carries."

Under the Government's reading of § 924(c)(1), "use" includes even the action of a defendant who puts a gun into place to protect drugs or to embolden himself. This reading is of such breadth that no role remains for "carry."

...

We assume that Congress used two terms because it intended each term to have a particular, nonsuperfluous meaning. While a broad reading of "use" undermines virtually any function for "carry," a more limited, active interpretation of "use" preserves a meaningful role for "carries" as an alternative basis for a charge. Under the interpretation we enunciate today, a firearm can be used without being carried, e. g., when an offender has a gun on display during a transaction, or barters with a firearm without handling it; and a firearm can be carried without being used, e. g., when an offender keeps a gun hidden in his clothing throughout a drug transaction.

Bailey v. United States, 516 U.S. 137 (1995)

6.4 Conclusion

Our look in this chapter at characteristics of legal discourses has included lexical properties, syntactic-semantic rules and tendencies, and law-specific "canons" of interpretation. Lexically, law discourse is full of jargon, including law-specific words like *plaintiff,* French and Latin words, and familiar English words with law-specific meanings like *action.* Syntactic-semantic rules and tendencies include using full NPs instead of pronouns for co-reference, use of *said* as a determiner and an adjective, and anaphoric use of *here* and *there* with suffixed prepositions, as well as lots of long, syntactically complex sentences, lots of passives (especially agentless ones), and uses of third person expressions in contexts where most non-law discourses would use first- and second-person pronouns. Linguistic canons of interpretation include *Noscitur a sociis* ("It is known by its neighbors"), *ejusdem generis* ("Of the same kind"), the Last Antecedent Rule, the Series Qualifier Rule, *Expressio unius est exclusio alterius* ("Expression of one thing is exclusion of another"), and the No Surplusage Rule. In addition, there's the Rule of Lenity, a meta-canon requiring disambiguation to favor defendants.

Some of these are specific to law: the jargon, the anaphoric use of full NPs instead of pronouns, and the canons. Others are patterns or uses found in formal discourses outside of law: anaphoric *said,* long and complicated sentences, passives, and third person uses instead of first and second.

So is there a "language" of the law? No, because the overwhelming majority of sentences used in legal discourses are constructed and understood entirely according to the morphological, syntactic, and semantic rules of English. Legal jargon may create some unintelligibility to non-law folks, just as with any specialized field, without implying the existence of a different language. But the law-specific rules, in particular the canons, impose law-specific interpretations which English speakers uninitiated into law can't be expected to predict. If these law-specific rules were pervasive, applying to most legal discourses, inferring the existence of legal English as a language would make sense, but they aren't; the canons apply pretty rarely. Here's Peter Tiersma's (2006) take on the matter: "[I]t would be a gross mischaracterization to suggest that lawyers have a language of their own. But it would also be inaccurate to say that legal language is nothing more than formal written language with some additional technical vocabulary ...[I]t is somewhere between a separate language and ordinary English, and it is much closer to ordinary English than many people seem to think."

Chapter 7

Contracts

7.0 Introduction

You're planning a party. You need a supply of high-quality desserts. You know that your classmate Jane has a reputation for excellent baking. You meet with her and tell her you're interested in hiring her because you've heard what great cookies she bakes. She tells you she'll be glad to help out. You propose a deal: For $75, she'll supply six dozen high quality chocolate chip cookies, to be delivered by noon the day of the party. Jane agrees; you write up a simple contract – "Jane will supply six dozen high quality chocolate chip cookies for [your name]'s party on [date], for $75" – and you both sign and date it. The appointed day comes; Jane shows up as promised with cookies in a large bag. Jane is OK with your not paying her right away; she knows you're busy getting ready. Later, when you start putting the cookies on platters, you're disappointed to see that the cookies are just store-bought cookies. You feel cheated. When Jane shows up the next day asking for her $75, do you have to pay her?

Morally, you obviously have a case; you and Jane clearly understood that you were hiring her because of her reputation as a top-notch baker, and she failed to deliver the kind of high-quality cookies that you expected. When you tell her that there is no way you are paying her, she responds, "See you in small claims court." And she follows through, suing you for breach of contract. Does your moral position stand up in court? Is the contract legally enforceable?

7.1 Elements of contracts

You figure you might have two arguments in favor of not paying Jane: the cookies were not "high quality," and your conversations with Jane before you both signed the contract included your telling Jane that her reputation for baking was why you wanted her to provide the cookies, and her replying that she was glad to help out – evidence of the true nature of the deal. You hurry to consult your friend Nino, a third-year law student, to get his view. Nino tells you you're probably going to lose, explaining that (i) the vagueness of "high quality" probably will protect Jane, and (ii) generally, **extrinsic** evidence, that is, evidence outside the contract document, like pre-contract talk whose content is not written into the contract, is not part of the deal. (Remember the "parol evidence rule," introduced in Chapter 6.) Nino tells you that all the elements of an enforceable contract are present. He lays out the standard legal version of the requirements:

1   Elements of a contract

    i) an agreed exchange or a *bargain*;
    ii) a *benefit* accrued by the promisor;
    iii) a *detriment* incurred by the promisee; and
    iv) a *quid pro quo* or an equivalence in performances.

As for (i), you and Jane had an agreed-to bargain. As for (ii) and (iii), taking each of you and Jane in turn as "promisor" and "promisee," each of you stood to gain a benefit and incur a detriment. Your benefit was the cookies, Jane's was the $75; your detriment was the price you agreed to pay, the $75, and Jane's was providing the cookies. As for (iv), the idea is that the respective benefits and detriments constitute the elements of the "quid pro quo"; the $75 is *for* the cookies.

Shoot, you think, or maybe an expletive with a different vowel. You decide, probably rationally, that it's better to pay Jane now than to risk having to pay more as a result of the lawsuit. (Jane has threatened to seek more than the $75 in damages because of the stress and hassle involved in bringing the lawsuit.) Luckily, she accepts your check for $75, writes you a receipt for it, and you're done. And, you figure, you're done with her, too – never again will you contract with her for anything.

7.2 More about the legal nature of contracts

Because you're naturally curious, and Nino is a good guy, you decide to ask him more about contract law. The conversation goes like this:

7.2.1 A dialogue

YOU: OK, so would Jane and I have had a contract if I had just asked her to bring some cookies, as a friend, and she agreed?

NINO: Nope. The bit about "benefit" and "detriment" can be summed up in the word **consideration**, meaning something of value promised in return for the benefit. Every contract has to involve consideration. A promise without a corresponding consideration is no contract.

YOU: OK. So does this consideration have to be money? What if I ask someone – not Jane, of course, I'm done with her – to provide cookies for my party and in return I'll provide cookies for their party the following week?

NINO: Yeah, that would be a contract. It would help if you were specific about what kind of cookies and how many.

YOU: OK. You know, what really bothers me about Jane's lousy storebought cookies is that she had to know what our understanding was, you know, for good homemade cookies. Is there some general requirement for sincerity when two people make a contract?

NINO: An expectation. Suppose you and I contract for you to mow my lawn every week for the summer, for $600, to be paid at the end of the summer. I don't intend to pay you; rather, I'm planning to sell the property and skip town. If you can find me, you can sue me.

YOU: OK, that makes sense. You're saying that when people make a contract, they naturally expect each other to be sincere about it, and if they're not, the contract is still enforceable.

NINO. Right.

YOU: How about if we didn't write the contract, but just came to an oral agreement and shook on it?

NINO: Well, oral contracts for *services* can be valid. For sale of *goods*, oral contracts are OK only as long as the consideration is less than $500. For services there's no max.

YOU: OK, How about this: I tell someone that I'll bring six dozen cookies to their place if their sister will bring six dozen to my house a week later.

NINO: Depends. A contract has to be between the two parties, **offeror** and **offeree**. If the person you are talking to promises that their sister will bring the cookies, that'll work. The two considerations would be your promise and your addressee's promise. You've got a good legal imagination. Have you considered law school?

YOU: No, I'm not interested in fighting other people's battles. Yeah, that offeror-offeree bit is what I figured. It doesn't quite make sense that someone can promise someone else's behavior, though, does it?

NINO: Hm. Not really, I guess, but if the promisor can really guarantee the other person's behavior, maybe it can work. It's OK under contract law.

YOU: Weird. OK, suppose I'm the offeror. I offer someone – not Jane – $75 if they'll scour my kitchen. I make the offer in an email. I don't get a reply, but when I get home the person has just finished cleaning. And let's say it's a fine job. Of course I would pay him, but legally would I have to? He never accepted my offer.

NINO: It's a contract. This kind is called a **unilateral** contract. Your cleaner's acceptance of your offer was shown in his **performance**, that is, his cleaning your kitchen. You gotta pay him.

YOU: What if he hasn't finished? What if he's just getting started? Does he have to finish?

NINO: If he wants to get paid, yes. But get this: he doesn't have to finish. If he wants, he can walk, without violating the contract. He never explicitly accepted, see.

YOU: Wait. He can renege but I can't?

NINO: Right. You offered, he accepted, by starting to clean, so if he finishes you have to pay, but since he didn't explicitly accept, he hasn't made a commitment.

YOU: Huh. I think I get it. I'm a linguistics major, you know. At bottom contract formation involves speech acts. Offering is a speech act and so is the usual kind of acceptance, but accepting by performance isn't a speech act, so he can stop without penalty, but I'm stuck because I carried out the speech act of offering and he seems to have accepted by starting the work.

NINO: Exactly.

YOU: OK. Back to "consideration." How about if my parents offer me a bunch of money, say $10,000, when I turn 25 if I stay celibate and sober, no sex, no alcohol, until then? Is my abstaining from sex and alcohol "consideration?" Not that I'd do it. But would that be a contract?

NINO: Ha! Yes. You really SHOULD consider law school. You've described a famous case we read in Contracts class, *Hamer v. Sidway*. A dad made a deal with his son exactly like that, except that the amount of money was $5000, which at the time – nineteenth century – was a whole lot, well over a hundred thousand in today's money, and what the son had to abstain from was alcohol, tobacco, swearing, and playing cards or billiards for money. Like I said, it was a nineteenth century case. The court ruled that the son's abstaining counted as consideration that benefited the dad.

YOU: This is cool. So how about if I offer to sell you my very valuable comic book collection, which has been appraised at several thousand dollars, for one cent? If you take me up on this offer, and I later change my mind, can our apparent contract be enforced?

NINO: Good one! It depends. Generally courts don't judge the adequacy of consideration. But you've given me an extreme example. In contracts class we studied a case like this, another nineteenth century one, *Keller v. Holderman*, in which one guy had sold an old watch worth $15 to the other guy for $300. The second guy had written a $300 check but had no money in his account. The whole thing was a joke. The guy had intended to write something on the check to make it un-cashable, but he didn't. The first guy was an asshole and sued for the $300. The judge said Nope, no contract, because the supposed transaction was a "frolic and banter."

YOU: Cool! I owe you a six-pack, or at least a beer.

NINO: No you don't. My giving you all this information was a gift, not part of a contract.

YOU: I'll buy you a six-pack anyway. I want to know more about these frolics and banters. In that case about the watch, it was obvious that the deal was a joke, right? Obvious to all, and the guy trying to enforce it knew it too?

NINO: Right.

YOU: So what if it's not clear? You know my car, my Mustang? It's worth, what, maybe $15,000. Suppose I offer to sell it to you for $1500. You jump at the offer, right?

NINO: For sure. This kind of contract has to be written, because it's for a sale of goods for more than $500, so we fill in one of those DMV forms or just write "[Your name] agrees to sell 2016 Mustang convertible, VIN 123456789, to Nino Scolio, for $1500." Next day I come over to your house, check in hand, to pick up my new ride. You refuse to accept the check and refuse to hand over the car key, saying "Come on, you know I was kidding." Well, if I say "No way, I took you at your word and we signed a contract," and take you to court to enforce the contract, if I can prove that a reasonable person in my position would have taken you seriously, I'd win - like if I can supply evidence of your demeanor (tone of voice, etc.), or your need for cash, or if I know you have a big gambling debt and Bruno the enforcer is threatening to break your thumbs, or maybe I know about your lack of sophistication in business or just ignorance of car values. On the other hand, if you could prove that I knew you were joking, like if you could find an email I wrote to my girlfriend right after signing the contract saying I knew you were joking but I intended to try to enforce the deal anyway, you'd win.

YOU: Huh. So it comes down to what the contract says, and what a reasonable person would think, eh?

NINO: Yeah. A famous character, this reasonable person. Shows up a lot in law. In the context of contracts, this approach is known as the **objective theory of contracts**. One party's secret intention or subjective understanding is irrelevant.

YOU: Beer. No, wait. One more. Let's say there's a reward on campus for info leading to the arrest and conviction of a vandal. Say someone spray painted political messages all over College Hall and the Admin Building. Reward of $10,000. If I know who did it and turn him in and he gets convicted, I get the reward, right? This is a unilateral contract?

NINO: Yep.

YOU: What if I'm a campus cop? It's my job to catch campus criminals. But the posters advertising the reward didn't exclude campus cops from eligibility for the reward.

NINO: You're out of luck. The rule is that a person with a **pre-existing duty** can't use performing the duty as consideration for the reward. Get it? Remember, every contract involves a benefit and a detriment, for each party. Jane supplied cookies. That was her detriment. Her benefit was the $75 you paid her. Your benefit was the cookies and your detriment was the $75. In the case of a police officer, like you said, it's his job to catch criminals. So he can't count catching this one as a detriment. If you're the campus cop, you didn't supply any consideration.

YOU: OK, now, beer.

7.2.2 Mutual mistake

Sometimes the parties to a contract both learn, after they have signed the contract, that what they thought about the subject matter of the contract was wrong, in a way greatly disadvantageous to one party and advantageous to the other. Here are a couple of famous nineteenth century examples:

In *Wood v. Boynton,* an 1885 Wisconsin case, a person sold a buyer a "stone," which both parties thought, but weren't sure, was a topaz, for one dollar. It turned out later that the stone was a diamond, worth about $700. The seller wanted to cancel the sale, but after a trial the court said No, on the grounds that there was no dispute over the identity of the stone, and inadequacy of price was not a good reason to rescind the contract.

In *Sherwood v. Walker,* an 1887 Michigan case, a person sold a cow. Both seller and buyer thought the cow (named, amazingly, "Rose 2d of Aberlone") was barren, and therefore good only for beef. Before the buyer took possession, Rose turned out to be not only fertile but pregnant, raising her intrinsic value by a factor of nine or ten. The seller refused to deliver Rose, and this time the court allowed rescission of the sale, holding that a fertile cow was "a thing different in substance" from what was bargained for and agreed to.

If you can't see a way to distinguish these two cases, you're not alone. How a fertile cow is a substantially different thing from a barren one but a diamond isn't a substantially different thing from a topaz is hard, or impossible, for anyone to see. Semantics is no help. In both cases the referent was clear: the stone and the cow. In both, each party was mistaken in the same way over the nature – or a very relevant property – of the thing. The judges in the two cases just described the reality differently, as a different thing "in substance" (cow) and as not (stone).

The only difference – a situational one – turns out to be the level of conviction in the mistaken beliefs. In the case of Rose the cow, both parties felt sure Rose was barren. In the stone case, both parties believed, but weren't sure, that the stone was just a topaz. The contract law principle goes like this: If a party knows their knowledge is limited but proceeds to agree to a contract on the assumption that that knowledge is sufficient, that party bears the risk of the incomplete knowledge. So the seller of the probable topaz that turned out to be a diamond was out of luck, but the seller of Rose the pregnant cow wasn't, because he was (mistakenly) very confident that Rose was barren.

Contract law is full of cases about mutual mistaken assumptions. A painting is sold for peanuts but later turns out to be the work of a famous artist and worth millions (*Nelson v. Rice,* 2000). A builder contracts with a landowner to build a house on the landowner's property. It turns out that the subsoil conditions are very rocky, making the project way more difficult and expensive than either party figured (*Watkins & Sons v. Carrig,* 1941). In both of these cases, the risk was assigned to the party with greater opportunity to know the truth, and, therefore, greater responsibility to. In the painting case, the seller was an estate of a deceased person, the buyer a non-expert. The estate executors had hired an appraiser who blew it in appraising the painting. Even though the appraiser had disclaimed any art expertise, the court held that the estate executors had had the chance to hire an expert art appraiser but didn't, so the risk, and the loss, was theirs. In the rocky subsoil case, the builder, because of his profession, was presumed to have greater knowledge of conditions which might make building difficult than the property owner. The builder was out of luck.

7.3 Speech act analysis

7.3.1 Contractual promises

Every contract is the result of an offer and an acceptance. We saw in the kitchen-scouring example above that acceptance can be accomplished by performance, but usually it's done by a speech act, just as offering is. Specifically, both are *promises,* conditional ones, the condition for each promise being the other contracting party's (equally conditional) promise. Here are felicity conditions for contractual promises:

2   Felicity conditions for contractual promises

Semantic content:	Future act A by Speaker.
Preparatory conditions:	(i) Addressee would prefer Speaker's doing act A to his not doing act A, and Speaker knows this.
	(ii) It is not obvious to both Speaker and Addressee that Speaker will do A in the normal course of events.
	(iii) Speaker has ability to do A.
	(iv) Addressee promises future act B by Addressee, with corresponding Preparatory Conditions (i–iv), i.e., including one corresponding to this one.
Essence:	Speaker intends that his utterance obligates him to do A.

The semantic content captures the fact that promises are about a future act. (The "act" can be a refraining, as in the example in the dialogue of refraining from sex and drugs.) Even though speakers sometimes use the verb *promise* loosely to swear that a statement about the past is true – "I promise I gave it to him" – doing so carries out a different speech act, asserting. The first Preparatory Condition distinguishes promises from threats, both involving future acts that affect an addressee, threats being about acts the Addressee wouldn't like, promises being about acts the Addressee would like. The second defines promises so as to exclude "promises" to do what one already will do; a promise is about a *new* obligation. Example: Mom always makes her son's lunch for school. It would be strange for her to say to her son "I promise to make your lunch tomorrow." The third rules out "promises" the speaker cannot carry out ("I promise to take you on a faster-than-light rocket ride to Mars tomorrow"). The fourth Preparatory Condition makes this kind of promise contingent on a reciprocal promise by Addressee. There are other kinds of contingent promises, like "I promise to take you to the movies if my parents let me have the car." Such contingent promises are not contractual promises. Contractual promises are always contingent on reciprocal promises from the other contracting party.

Notice that there's no sincerity condition, on the theory that contracts – binding ones – can be made by promisors who have no intent to carry out their part of the bargain. Our fictitious law student Nino pointed this out in the dialogue above. The "Essence" is consistent with this; the speaker intends to undertake the obligation, regardless of their intent to fulfill it. This understanding of contractual promises is consistent with contracting parties' assumptions about each other's good faith in forming the contract, but insincerity won't invalidate an otherwise good contract.

The felicity conditions in (2) are not the whole story about contracts; they just describe the mutually conditioning promises. The elements of contracts listed in (1) include element (iii), the detriment to the promisor. With that in mind consider this scenario: Suzanne, a mediocre student with mediocre test scores, applies for admission to Caltech. Her dad says "If you are admitted to Caltech, I'll give you a BMW convertible." Suzanne replies, "Deal!" Is this a contract? No. Here's why. Imagine that miraculously Suzanne gets in. Her getting in to Caltech was fortuitous; she didn't give up anything in return for the promised convertible. She incurred no detriment. Therefore, there was no contract. To be sure, if Dad doesn't give her the BMW, Suzanne has every right to be angry; Dad broke a promise. But a promise is not necessarily a contract.

Contrast a different scenario: Suzanne applies to Caltech and to San Diego State. She is accepted by both. Her dad says "If you go to Caltech, I'll give you a BMW convertible." Suzanne replies, "Deal!" She chooses Caltech. Does her Dad have to give her the BMW? Yes: This time Suzanne has incurred a detriment, namely foregoing her opportunity to matriculate at San Diego State. There is a contract; she's entitled to the car. Too bad she'll be too busy studying to enjoy it.

7.3.2. Offer and acceptance

A contract is formed by an offer and an acceptance. Except for unilateral contracts, like the example in the dialogue of hiring a person to scour your kitchen, both are speech acts, specifically promises. (A unilateral contract is accepted by performance, not by a promise.) Linguist Sanford Schane (2012) distinguishes between "autonomous" and "cooperative" speech acts. Autonomous ones are effective instantly, with no response required from an addressee. Examples: congratulating someone, appointing someone, asserting something, warning someone – and flatly promising: "I promise to bring cookies to your party." Cooperative speech acts require a response before they become effective. Example: betting. Suppose you say to a friend "I'll bet you $100 the Red Sox will beat the Yankees tomorrow night." There's no bet unless and until your friend responds with an uptake: saying "You're on!," or "OK!," or otherwise signaling agreement to the bet. What you said to your friend was actually an *offer* to bet. Just as there's no bet without uptake, there's no contract without acceptance. Specifically, a contractual offer is a promise, but a contingent or conditional one, not a flat one. Offering to bet $100 on the Red Sox beating the Yankees in tomorrow's game is a promise to pay the addressee $100 if the Yankees win, in return for the addressee's promise to pay you $100 if the Red Sox win. The speech act nature of contractual offers and acceptances can be summarized in their felicity conditions. First, offers:

3   Felicity conditions for contractual offers

Semantic content:	Future contract K between Offeror and Offeree.
Preparatory conditions:	(i) Contract K has all the elements of contracts.
	(ii) It is not obvious to both Offeror and Offeree that Offeror will perform his part of contract K in the normal course of events.
	(iii) Offeror has ability to perform his part of contract K.
Essence:	Offeror intends that his utterance obligates him to form contract with Offeree if Offeree accepts.

Preparatory condition (i) includes the elements listed in (1), at the beginning of the chapter, namely an agreed exchange, a benefit to the promisor, a detriment to the promisee, and a quid pro quo relationship between the respective benefits and detriments. Preparatory condition (ii) excludes pre-existing duties and other acts that would occur without the contract. Preparatory condition (iii) rules out performances that are impossible.

Acceptances are identical to offers except for their Essence:

4   Felicity conditions for acceptances of contractual offers

Semantic content:	Future contract K between Offeror and Offeree.

Preparatory conditions:	(i) Contract K has all the elements of contracts.
	(ii) It is not obvious to both Offeror and Offeree that Offeree will perform her part of contract K in the normal course of events.
	(iii) Offeree has ability to perform her part of contract K.
Essence:	Offeree intends that her utterance obligates her to form contract with Offeror.

The Essence of a contractual acceptance, unlike an offer, is unconditional.

Often an offer is not accepted as presented. An offeree who is interested in getting a deal with the offeror can counter-offer, changing the roles of the parties; now the original offeree is the offeror, and the original offeror is the offeree. There is no limit on how many times this can occur. Back-and-forth counter-offers are the formalization of negotiations. It's important, though, to distinguish exploratory or preliminary negotiations from actual (counter-) offers. While the difference might not be clear in practice, the difference is real, and can be understood in speech act terms. Exploring possibilities – "Maybe, if you give me odds, like say 6–5 or so" – in reply to the offer to bet on the game – has the speech act nature of a question or an assertion, whereas an actual counter-offer has the nature of a promise. "Deal, if you'll give me 6–5 odds" is a counter-offer. The form of an utterance may not guarantee which we have: "How about if you give me 6–5 odds" might count as a counter-offer, or might not. Successful (or overbearing) salespeople often try to get customers to commit to offers:

Salesperson: What do you think?
Customer: I like it but I'm concerned about the price.
Salesperson: Would you buy it if I could get the price under $20K?

At this point any affirmative response by the customer is likely to be met by the salesman's "OK!" and outstretched hand. It's hard not to shake a hand offered for a shake. The salesman's next line might be "Congratulations!" accompanied by a big dose of charm and reassurance to overcome any bewilderment or unsureness on the part of the customer, who may not have actually been ready to seal the deal.

7.4 Ambiguity

There are lots of fascinating issues with contracts that are not linguistic in nature. Since this book is about linguistics and law, we'll stick to contract issues that are linguistic. The nature of contracts as being reciprocal conditioned and conditioning promises can be understood through speech act theory, as we saw above. A different area of linguistics, semantics, can illuminate a recurring problem between parties to a contract: ambiguity. Usually the ambiguity in a problem contract is accidental and unforeseen. But our first example, a real one, involves purposeful ambiguity. The ambiguity was phonological. The location was a Hooters restaurant in Panama City, Florida. The *dramatis personae* were the Hooters manager, Jared Blair, and Hooters waitresses, including one named Jodee Berry. Manager Blair organized a contest among the waitresses to see who could sell the most beer. The ten who did would be entered into a drawing. The winner would be blindfolded and led out to the parking lot to her new [tʰojoɾa], [ɾ] being a **tap**, the everyday, casual pronunciation of both the /t/ in *latter* and the /d/ in *ladder*. So [tʰojoɾa] is phonologically ambiguous between /tojota/ and /tojoda/, i.e., *Toyota* and *toy Yoda*. Jodee Berry won. When she removed her blindfold, she was presented with a brand-new toy Yoda doll, Yoda being the *Star Wars* character. Joke! Ha! Ha! Ms. Berry sued. At trial extrinsic evidence was allowed in, including statements by manager Blair that the prize might be a truck, car, or van, but he knew it would be a new [tʰojoɾa], and that the winner would be responsible for sales tax on it. Apparently, Blair had been careful only to implicate, not literally assert, that the prize would be a Toyota automobile. The case was settled. Ms. Berry received an undisclosed sum, enough, according to her attorney, to buy any kind of Toyota she wanted.

Here are the facts of another case, a famous one. A nineteenth century contract between two businessmen was about the purchase and delivery of a shipload of cotton from India. The contract detailed the kind of cotton, the quantity (125 bales), the price, the port of origin (Bombay), and the name of the ship, *Peerless*. When the *Peerless* arrived at Liverpool, England, and the cotton was unloaded, the purchasing businessman refused to accept it and pay. It turned out there were two ships named *Peerless*, both involved in India-Great Britain trade, one which had left Bombay in October – with no cotton for the purchaser – and one which left in December, this one with the cotton for the purchaser. The purchaser had had the earlier-leaving *Peerless* in mind when he signed the contract, and was ready to pay for the cotton that he had expected to arrive on that ship; the seller had had the later-leaving *Peerless* in mind. The purchaser presumably got his cotton from another source or did something else with the money he had originally budgeted to pay for the cotton that didn't arrive on the *Peerless* he had in mind. When he refused to pay for the cotton that arrived on the second *Peerless*, the seller sued.

The facts of this case have to do with the meaning of names. A name, fundamentally, has a simple meaning: just its referent. The referent of *Bombay* is that city (now known as *Mumbai*), and that's all *Bombay* literally means. Other things about the place, such as its location (west coast of India), its rank as largest city of India, its role in finance and in the Indian film industry, etc., sometimes identified as "associated components" of meaning, can usefully be separated from the literal meaning, namely, its referent, the city itself. *George* means an individual named George, known to the speaker, and, presumably, to the addressee. Other than that, it has hardly any meaning (just the fact that it's a name, and it's usually used to refer to males rather than females). The fact that there are lots of Georges in the world doesn't matter. If you and I know one of them, we can use *George* to refer to him. The individual referred to, the referent of the word in our (possibly little) speech community, is all the word means when we use it to talk about the George we know. Even if we know more than one George, our talk about one of them will almost always create a tacit understanding about which one we are referring to. The meanings of common nouns are much more complicated. By themselves they have no reference, although of course a noun phrase containing a common can be used to refer to something: The noun *apple* has, by itself, no reference, but *the apple* can refer to some particular apple. Common nouns have *meaning*, of course, learnable from dictionary definitions or **ostensive** (pointing) acts like what might accompany the utterance "THAT is an apple." By the way, dictionary definitions are not meanings; they're just paraphrases of a word. It turns out that to specify precisely the meaning of a word like *apple* is complicated. That meaning doesn't even contain much, if any, botanical information, on the theory that word meanings are (unconsciously) known by speakers, and speakers know the meaning of the word without having to know much, if anything, about apples' botanical nature. Fortunately, the meaning of *names,* like the name *Peerless* in the cotton shipment case, is simple: the word's referent only.

How would you decide the two-ships-named-*Peerless* case, if you were the judge? Looking at the felicity conditions for conditional promises, given in (2) above, won't help; what needs to be filled out is the nature of "Future Act A," what the cotton buyer was bound by the contract to do: pay for the cotton, sure enough, but what cotton? The cotton he had in mind, which didn't show up, or the cotton the seller had in mind, which did?

Here's how the court that heard the case decided it:

5   A latent ambiguity appeared when the contract did not specify which '*Peerless*' was intended. There is nothing on the face of the contract to show that any particular ship called *Peerless* was meant but the moment it appears that two ships called the *Peerless* were about to sail from Bombay, there is a latent ambiguity. Parol evidence will be admissible for determining the actual meaning that each party assigned to that

ambiguity. From the evidence presented, each party attached a different meaning to that ambiguity. If different meanings were intended on a material term of a contract, there is no mutual assent and there is no contract.

Raffles v Wichelhaus 2 H. & C. 906, 159 Eng. Rep. 373
(Ex. 1864)

So, the court said, if there's a "latent" ambiguity, parol evidence is allowed in as evidence, and if it turns out that the two parties had different referents in mind, there was no actual mutual agreement and therefore no contract.

Contrasting with latent ambiguities are **patent** ones, ambiguities observable directly in the contract. Imagine a contractual promise to pay a certain amount, when the amount is stated as different sums in different parts of the contract. Suppose, for example, that you agree on a contract to sell your bike for a certain price. The contract document has "two hundred dollars" written in one place and "$20.00" written in another place. The contradiction creates a patent ambiguity. You'd think the resolution of the ambiguity would be easy: just admit testimony about the respective intentions of you and the buyer, and if there's disagreement, admit testimony about the value of the bike under current market conditions. Under the traditional rule, *Nope*: extrinsic evidence is excluded in the case of patent ambiguities, and – hopefully – there will be some principle available to resolve the issue. In the case of a clash of this sort, there is: the words trump the figures, on the theory that writers are less likely to err writing words than figures. Two hundred dollars, not 20, for the bike. In other cases, what may apply is the rule *fortius contra proferentem,* "more strongly against the profferor," that is, against the offeror, a rule akin to the rule of lenity in criminal law. How this rule works can be seen when there is unequal bargaining power, such as in a typical retail context. A retail store offers to sell things, for a price that it sets. Most of the time the store has greater bargaining power than a customer; imagine at checkout in a grocery store trying to negotiate the prices of your groceries. If the store mistakenly marks the price of an item lower than it had planned, generally it's stuck and has to sell the item at the marked price.

Today, most jurisdictions ignore the "latent" – "patent" distinction and admit extrinsic evidence to resolve contractual ambiguities. Whether a contract is ambiguous is sometimes not obvious. A judge can be asked to determine whether a contract that appears unambiguous on its face actually is subject to different interpretations. In such a situation the judge would almost certainly have to listen to – i.e., admit as evidence – extrinsic evidence such as testimony about the parties' intentions or common practice in business deals of the same kind. The clash between the traditional approach and the modern approach was nicely captured in the trial court decision and its appellate reversal in a 1968 California case. Pacific Gas & Electric (PG&E) hired an outside contractor, the Thomas Drayage Co., to repair a broken cover on a steam generator. During the repair work the cover fell and damaged another part, a rotor, to the tune of over $25,000. Under the contract the Drayage Co. **indemnified** PG&E against" all loss, damage, expense and liability resulting from ... injury to property, arising out of or in any way connected with the performance of this contract." *Indemnify* means "financially protect from loss," that is, in this case, pay for damage. At trial, Drayage argued that the indemnification words in the contract were intended to cover damage only to third parties' property, and tried to introduce evidence to that effect from statements by PG&E, from Drayage's behavior under contracts like this one (with PG&E, even), and from other evidence. The trial judge agreed that the contract wording was "the classic language for a third party indemnity provision," but applied the traditional view that the words of a contract were binding if there was no "ambiguity" on its face. The contract said "all...property"; end of story. No extrinsic evidence was allowed in. Drayage was responsible. On appeal, the opposite approach was taken. Reversing the trial court, the appellate court began from the assumption that any contract represented the intentions of the parties and needed to be interpreted on the basis of that assumption. The court then offered some observations about the meaning of words used in contracts:

6   When the court interprets a contract [as the trial court did], it determines [its] meaning ... in accordance with the "... extrinsic evidence of the judge's own linguistic education and experience." (cite omitted).

...

A rule that would limit the determination of the meaning of a written instrument to its [content alone] merely because it seems to the court to be clear and unambiguous, would either deny the relevance of the intention of the parties or presuppose a degree of verbal precision and stability our language has not attained.

...

The meaning of particular words or groups of words varies with the "... verbal context and surrounding circumstances and purposes in view of the linguistic education and experience of their users and their hearers or readers (not excluding judges)." (cite omitted) ... [T]he meaning of a writing "... can only be found by interpretation in the light of all the circumstances that reveal the sense in which the writer used the words. The exclusion of parol evidence regarding such circumstances merely because the words do not appear ambiguous to the reader can easily lead to the attribution to a written instrument of a meaning that was never intended." (cites omitted)

...

The fact that the terms of an instrument appear clear to a judge does not preclude the possibility that the parties chose the language of the instrument to express different terms.

Pacific Gas & Electric Co. v. G.W. Thomas Drayage and Rigging Co., 442 P.2d 641 (Cal. 1968)

7.5 Conclusion

In this chapter we've looked at the nature of contracts from the legal perspective and, in more detail, from the standpoint of semantics and speech act theory. Fundamentally a contract is a pair of mutually conditioned and conditioning promises. Beyond that speech act nature, contracts have legal requirements, in particular consideration (detriment and value, to both parties). Semantic interpretation issues arise with ambiguities of reference (as in the *Peerless* case) and (rarely) of phonology (the toy Yoda case). A foundational question is whether the intentions of the contracting parties or the words of the contract should rule (*PG&E v. Drayage*). In the next chapter we'll see a similar issue arise with respect to the interpretation of statutes and the Constitution.

Chapter 8

Statutory and constitutional interpretation

8.0 Introduction

8.0.1 Contracts vs. legislation

Let's start by comparing legislation with contracts. Both are **operative**; they *do* something. In both, the same sort of issues arise when they are fought over in court: What does the language mean? How do they apply to unforeseen situations? What was the intent of the signatories or enactors?

But the differences are big. When a court has to interpret a contract, almost always the contract makers are the ones fighting, so they're available to tell the court their stories about intent. Often when a statute has to be interpreted by a court, this happens long after the statute was enacted, so the enactors aren't all around. Worse, with contracts, each party to the contract almost certainly had a clear intent about the contract, but the "intent" behind a piece of legislation is a fiction, since legislators are not a collective mind; rather, they're individuals with individual, often inconsistent intents.

8.0.2 Unforeseen situations

Imagine a city ordinance that bars vehicles from a park, a famous (and made-up) example (Hart & Sacks 1958). So you can't drive your car in, or your ATV, or your motorcycle, but what about your bicycle? If riding it in violates the ordinance, what about walking it in? Can kids bring tricycles? Scooters? Skateboards? Roller skates? Wheeled shoes that kids wear – "heelies?" Can a mom bring a baby carriage? A homeless guy his shopping cart? Is a wheelchair permitted? A motorized one? Can a trash disposal company send in a garbage truck? Suppose somebody in the park needs immediate medical assistance. Can an ambulance come in? How about a large toy truck that a child might push around laden with smaller toys? Would it be different if the toy truck carried not toys, but a smaller sibling?

What about the reason for the law? Is it safety? Or noise abatement? Should the reason affect the interpretation?

You might think common sense would supply answers, but one person's common sense might not be another's, and there may be examples for which common sense doesn't supply an answer. If you were the judge who had to decide any of these cases, on what basis should you rule? Are there general principles? In this chapter first we'll look at some different such principles, then some examples involving interpretive problems from different levels of linguistic structure, *syntax* and *the lexicon* (that is, words).

8.1 Theories of statutory interpretation

Introducing statutory interpretation, Eskridge, Frickey, and Garrett (2007) identify three approaches: "**intentionalism**, in which the interpreter identifies and then follows the original intent of the statute's drafters, **purposivism**, in which the interpreter chooses the interpretation that best carries out the statutes' purpose; and **textualism**, in which the interpreter follows the "plain meaning" of the statute's text" (2007: 690). Yes, the distinction between intentionalism and purposivism is subtle, and while real, it will be largely ignored in our discussion to follow.

The most influential theory of statutory interpretation was until around the turn of the century a purposivist one, Hart & Sacks' (1958) "**legal process**" theory, which defined the job of interpretation as deciding "what meaning ought to be given" to a statute by attributing a purpose to the legislature's enactment, using legislative history and considering what problem the statute was designed to address, without, however, giving "the words … a meaning they will not bear" (Eskridge, Frickey, & Garrett, *op. cit.*). We will see below that this tether to the language is not always present in opinions whose arguments comport with the legal process theory.

As an example of purposivism/intentionalism, consider a case well known to students of statutory meaning, the 1892 Supreme Court case *Rector, etc., of Holy Trinity Church v. U.S.* The church had hired an English pastor, in apparent violation of a federal statute with the following language:

1 [I]t shall be unlawful…to prepay the transportation, or in any way assist or encourage the importation or migration of any alien…into the United States…, under contract…to perform labor or service of any kind in the United States…

Act of Feb. 26, 1885, 23 Stat. 32, c. 164 (cited in case)

Taking this language seriously, the Court said:

2 It must be conceded that the act of the corporation is within the letter of this section, for the relation of rector to his church is one of service, and implies labor on the one side with compensation on the other. Not only are the general words labor and service both used, but also, as it were to guard against any narrow interpretation and emphasize a breadth of meaning, to them is added "of any kind;" …

Rector, etc., of Holy Trinity Church v. U.S.,
143 U.S. 457 (1892)

But, the Court held, in frequently quoted language:

3 It is a familiar rule, that a thing may be within the letter of the statute and yet not within the statute, because not within its spirit, nor within the intention of its makers.

Id.

The Court went on to argue that an absurd result of applying a statute literally "makes it unreasonable to believe that the legislator intended to include the particular act." The absurd result in this case would be prohibiting the importation of "ministers of the gospel, or, indeed, of any class whose toil is that of the brain." According to the Court, the problem that the statute addressed was the depressing effect on the labor market caused by the importation of "an ignorant and servile class of foreign laborers." The Court thus recognized the linguistic meaning of the statutory language, but asserted that the legal rule supposedly encoded in the statute was not well encoded in its words, having, instead, a "spirit" that the Court was bound to figure out – a sort of Platonic view of statutes. In sum, the Court assumed that what mattered was Congress's intent, and decided that the legislative intent must have been such-and-such, because of the problem that the statute was enacted to remedy – regardless of what the statute said.

Contrasting with purposivism is textualism. The leading proponent of textualism in the late 20th and early 21st centuries was the late Justice Antonin Scalia:

4 It is the *law* that governs, not the intent of the lawgiver…[I]t is only the laws that they enact which bind us.

 …

 [I]f … the object of judicial interpretation is to determine the intent of the legislature, .. the practical threat is that… judges will in fact pursue their own objectives and desires…When you are told to decide, not on the basis of what the legislature said, but on the basis of what it *meant,* … your best shot at figuring out what the legislature meant is to ask yourself what a wise and intelligent person *should* have meant; and that will surely bring you to the conclusion that the law means what you think it *ought* to mean…

Scalia 1997, 17–18

Judges are supposed to *apply* the law, not *make* it. That's for the legislature. Judicial law-making violates separation of powers.

Scalia was unforgiving about *Holy Trinity*: "Well of course I think that the act was within the letter of the statute, and was therefore within the statute: end of case. Congress can enact foolish statutes as well as wise ones, and it is not for the courts to decide which is which and rewrite the former" (*id*.: 20).

In addition, textualists argue, legislative intent is elusive: as suggested above, legislators have a wide range of "intents" when they design or vote for a bill – to support a party or the President, to repay a favor, to exact revenge, to seek favor from voters, etc. Outside pressures from lobbyists and interest groups are powerful motivators too: Legislation is often enacted through compromise and deal-making; sometimes what gets included in or excluded from a bill is "consideration" (in the contract sense!) for a corresponding consideration in a different bill, or for something else political. And modern legislation is often long. The 2001 "No Child Left Behind Act" was 274,000 words long. President Obama's "Affordable Care Act" was over 300,000 words long. When a long statute is enacted, few legislators have read the whole thing, and often don't fully know what they're voting for.

So what about abstracting away from actual individual legislators' intents to some "objective intent" embodied in the legislation? Such purpose might be ascertained from public discourse (newspapers, TV and radio opinion, blogs, etc.) about a problem, and from legislative history: committee reports, hearings, floor debates, and public statements by legislators. According to Scalia, looking for purpose/intent in such sources can lead to mistaken conclusions because

[5]   Nowadays, when it is universally known and expected that judges will resort to floor debates and (especially) committee reports as authoritative expressions of "legislative intent," affecting the courts rather than informing the Congress has become the primary purpose of the exercise. It is less that the courts refer to legislative history because it exists than that legislative history exists because the courts refer to it.

Id., 34

Plus there's no algorithm, no rules governing what weight different elements of legislative history deserve. Scalia quotes a judge as saying that looking at legislative history is like a cocktail party: "The trick is to look over the heads of the crowd and pick out your friends" (*id.:* 36).

Even farther removed from statutory language than legislative intent or purpose is public policy, or, more broadly (and ambitiously), justice. The heck with the stability and predictability that presumably comes from textualism. Let judges revise statutory laws that have become out of date or in conflict with current values. This is what judges do with non-statutory law – **common law** – cases. (A lot of law in the areas of contracts and property is common, rather than statutory, law; criminal law is almost entirely statutory.) Since legislatures move slowly, according to this "consider public policy and do justice" view, courts should be able to change even statutory law when it produces unjust results. Important writings favoring this approach include Calabresi 1982 and Eskridge 1994.

A 1990 Supreme Court case, *Maryland v. Craig,* provides a good example of a clash between a public policy concern and textualism. In this case, a child was a witness against a defendant accused of sexually abusing her. The child was allowed to give her testimony without the presence of the defendant, in a separate room with judge, prosecutor, and defense attorney present, but not the defendant. The defendant could observe the child's testimony on TV, but the child would be spared having to see the defendant. The defendant, a pre-school teacher named Sandra Ann Craig, was convicted. She appealed, arguing that she had been deprived of her Sixth Amendment right to "be confronted with the witnesses against [her]." She lost. **You should now read *Maryland v. Craig.*** Here are snippets from Justice Sandra Day O'Connor's majority opinion and Justice Scalia's dissent:

6   O'Connor: [U]se of the one-way closed-circuit television procedure, where necessary to further an important state interest, does not impinge upon the truth-seeking or symbolic purposes of the Confrontation Clause.

Scalia: The Court has convincingly proved that the Maryland procedure serves a valid interest, and gives the defendant virtually everything the Confrontation Clause guarantees (everything, that is, except confrontation). I am persuaded, therefore, that the Maryland procedure is virtually constitutional. Since it is not, however, actually constitutional, I would [reverse] the judgment of conviction.

Maryland v. Craig, 496 U.S. 836 (1990)

The majority followed a public policy rationale. Scalia argued for sticking to the plain meaning of the language of the provision.

Scalia also argued for a limited role of the judiciary with respect to Constitutional provisions that might be considered defective:

[7]   I have no need to defend the value of confrontation, because the Court has no authority to question it. It is not within our charge to speculate that, "where face-to-face confrontation causes significant emotional distress in a child witness," confrontation might "in fact disserve the Confrontation Clause's truth-seeking goal." ... If so, that is a defect in the Constitution – which should be amended ... but cannot be corrected by judicial pronouncement that it is archaic [or] contrary to "widespread belief" .... For good or bad, the Sixth Amendment requires confrontation, and we are not at liberty to ignore it.

Id.

A purposivist might answer: "Get real! Amending the Constitution is very hard!" Scalia might reply: "Good!", and go on to point out that although one might be troubled by a textualist outcome in one case, there might be others where one would be relieved to see the language of a Constitutional provision prevent a change one opposed, or mandate a change one wanted.

8.2 Interpretation vs. construction

At this point it will be useful to draw an important distinction, first made by the nineteenth century scholar Francis Lieber (1839), and adapted and brought to linguists' attention by Peter Tiersma (1995). **Interpretation** of a statute or constitutional provision is a mental act, the psychological process of determining the ("linguistic") meaning of the words, phrases, and sentences making up the statute or provision, and the (again, "linguistic") meaning of the whole statute or provision. Interpretation involves determining not only the literal meaning of statutory language, but also what it implicates. Interpretation of statutes and constitutional provisions is therefore the same process that any person uses to comprehend anything they listen to or read. **Construction** (the noun formed from the verb *construe*), on the other hand, is the judicial act of saying what the *legal meaning* of a statute or provision is. Construction is **illocutionary**; put simply, it's a speech act. In Searle's (1975) classification, it's a **declaration**, that is, a speech act that changes the world by bringing into existence the state of affairs encoded in its words. Other declarations are firing, resigning, appointing, sentencing, and christening. When a court construes a statute or provision, it makes its construal law. In principle, a court's construction is like a baseball umpire's call of "out" or "safe." The umpire observes the play and sees whether the runner is out or safe (akin to a court's interpreting a statute) and then rules the runner out or safe. The umpire might get it wrong, but the call stands, in other words creates reality.

The distinction between interpretation and construction may help contrast purposivism and "public policy-ism" with textualism. For a textualist judge the construction of a statute should be identical to its interpretation, or as near as possible; for a purposivist (etc.) judge in principle the construction can be pretty free, basically untethered to the interpretation. Arguments for purposivism typically don't go that far; as we saw above, the "legal process" approach did require that a construction of a statute not give words "a meaning they will not bear." But purposive (or public policy-oriented) judicial decision-making can deviate pretty far from the meaning of the language of a statute or constitutional provision, *Holy Trinity* and *Maryland v. Craig* being examples.

8.3 Originalism

Statutes and the Constitution are supposed to work indefinitely, unless they're repealed, amended, or found unconstitutional. For this relative permanence to exist, the meaning of a statute or constitutional provision has to remain constant. The problem is that today's world is so different from the world of a couple of hundred years ago that insisting on original meaning risks making old laws like the Constitution irrelevant. On the other hand, maybe abandoning original meaning allows judges to interpret a provision in light of their own values, an approach that makes an old statute or the Constitution just as irrelevant, in a different way.

Mainly the debate has been more about the Constitution than about statutes, so we'll focus on the Constitution.

This area is fraught. Legal scholars and judges have strong feelings about it. There are rough correlations between political conservatism and favoring originalism, and between political progressivism and seeing the Constitution as "living and breathing," although that metaphor is not used so much by non-originalists as by originalists excoriating them.

8.3.1 Originalism: pro

Justice Scalia was the most prominent advocate not only of textualism, but also of originalism:

8   Perhaps the most glaring defect of Living Constitutionalism... is that there is no agreement...upon what is to be the guiding principle of the evolution... [T]he evolutionists divide into as many camps as there are individual views of the good, the true, and the beautiful...

There is plenty of room for disagreement as to what original meaning was...But the originalist at least knows what he is looking for: the original meaning of the text....

[T]he difficulties and uncertainties of determining original meaning and applying it to modern circumstances are negligible compared with the difficulties and uncertainties of the philosophy which says that the Constitution *changes*...

Scalia 1997, 45

According to Scalia, when Constitutional language is ignored, the Constitution may be reduced to only a sort of cover term for a judge's personal values, or for courts becoming like legislatures following popular opinion. When this happens, disaster becomes possible:

9   If the courts are free to write the Constitution anew, they will, by God, write it the way the majority wants...This, of course, is the end of the Bill of Rights, whose meaning will be committed to the very body it was meant to protect against: the majority. By trying to make the Constitution do everything that needs doing from age to age, we shall have caused it to do nothing at all.

Id., 47

8.3.2 Originalism: con

One answer from non-originalists is that originalism risks preventing the court system, and the Court, from being able to counter majoritarian wrongful behavior. Law professor Erwin Chemerinsky argues that:

10 [An] emphasis on majoritarianism and judicial deference to the elected branches of government has no stopping point: ... Why have judicial review at all if ... elected officials are better equipped to determine the Constitution's meaning in modern circumstances ...?

Chemerinsky 2013, 948

"Majoritarianism" here means undue deference to legislation. Later in the same article Chemerinsky makes an argument about outcomes, ironically echoing the concern expressed by Scalia in ex. (9) above:

11   [It is important] to recognize the dangers of unchecked major-
     itarianism. When is the last time a legislature passed a law
     increasing the rights of criminal defendants or prisoners or enemy
     combatants? It is easy to romanticize self-government and demo-
     cratic rule, but it is precisely because of distrust of majoritarianism
     and a fear of its excesses that the Constitution was adopted.

Id., 951

Chemerinsky is worried about unchecked legislative majoritarianism, Scalia about courts becoming majoritarian.

8.3.3   Originalism: pro (take 2)

Above, in the middle paragraph of ex. (8), we saw Scalia's recognition that original meaning can be hard to ascertain. This suggests a
certain openness to the possibility of construing the Constitution a
new, still originalist, way. Law professor Steven Calabresi, like Scalia
an originalist, argues that some of the dramatic social Supreme Court
decisions of the 20th and early 21st century, like *Brown v. Board of
Education* (1954; outlawing school segregation), *Loving v. Virginia*
(1967; finding statutes forbidding mixed-race marriages unconstitutional), and *Obergefell v. Hodges* (2015; holding that gay couples'
marrying was a constitutional right) are justifiable on originalist
grounds, specifically on Fourteenth Amendment grounds (Calabresi
& Begley 2016; Calabresi undated). Notice, in the following, not just
the expansive originalism, but also the textualism:

12   Did one white citizen enjoy a common law or fundamental
     right to marry another white citizen of the opposite sex in
     1868? Of course ...The Fourteenth Amendment then says
     African Americans shall enjoy "the same right [or to be pre-
     cise privilege or immunity] ... as is enjoyed by white citi-
     zens." ...You cannot constitutionally give an "abridged," or

shortened, set of rights to some citizens as compared to others on the basis of their race. The text compels this answer. The fact that few people realized this at the time simply shows that Congress and the States did not understand what they had done when they enacted the Fourteenth Amendment. But it is not necessary that legislators understand what they have done when they enact a law anymore than it is necessary that individuals understand all aspects of what they have done when they sign a contract.

Calabresi and Fine Undated, 10–11

8.3.4 Originalism: con (take 2)

Arguing against originalism, former Seventh Circuit judge Richard Posner takes Scalia's admission that originalists can disagree over original meaning a step farther, saying that one reason originalism is problematic is that history is hard, and judges are not good historians:

13 The decisive objection to the quest for original meaning, even when the quest is conducted in good faith, is that judicial historiography rarely dispels ambiguity. Judges are not competent historians. Even real historiography is frequently indeterminate, as real historians acknowledge.

Posner 2012

Posner goes on to say that a judge's confidence in doing history can be dangerous:

14 To put to a judge a question that he cannot answer is to evoke "motivated thinking," the form of cognitive delusion that consists of credulously accepting the evidence that supports a preconception and of peremptorily rejecting the evidence that contradicts it.

Id.

This concern parallels Scalia's concern ((5) above) about judges interpreting statutes or the Constitution in light of their own values.

Some non-originalists argue that the way courts have actually construed Constitutional provisions is similar to the way they have decided common law cases: by sticking to precedent when they can, and creating new law when they have to, usually just incrementally. Law professor David Strauss puts it like this:

15   The common law is a system built not on an authoritative, foundational, quasi-sacred text like the Constitution. Rather, the common law is built out of precedents and traditions that accumulate over time. Those precedents allow room for adaptation and change, but only within certain limits and only in ways that are rooted in the past. Our constitutional system has become a common law system, one in which precedent and past practices are, in their own way, as important as the written Constitution itself...

      ...

      Most of the real work will be done by the Court's analysis of its previous decisions.

      ...

      Where the precedents leave off, or are unclear or ambiguous, the opinion will make arguments about fairness or good policy....

      ...

      Advocates know what actually moves the Court. Briefs are filled with analysis of the precedents and arguments about which result makes sense as a matter of policy or fairness. Oral argument in the Court works the same way. The text of the Constitution hardly ever gets mentioned. It is the unusual case in which the original understandings get much attention. In constitutional cases, the discussion at oral argument will be about the Court's previous decisions and, often, hypothetical questions designed to test whether a particular interpretation will lead to results that are implausible as a matter of common sense.

Strauss 2010

8.3.5 Interpreting vague provisions

A leading problem area in the battle between originalists and non-originalists is the Constitution's vague provisions, such as the Fourth Amendment's prohibition of "unreasonable searches and seizures," the Fifth and Fourteenth Amendment's guarantee of "due process," the Sixth Amendment's right to a "speedy" trial, the Eighth Amendment's ban on "cruel and unusual punishment," and the Fourteenth Amendment's guarantee of the "equal protection of the law." Non-originalists see these vague provisions as open-ended guarantees of rights, some unimagined by the enactors, whereas some originalists (not all; see (12) above) insist that rights not contemplated by enactors are not guaranteed by these provisions; rather, the original **public understanding** of the provisions was all they mean. The reason is the same concern that textualists say motivates them, that is, to ensure that judges do no more than apply the law, and refrain from introducing their own values into the judging process. And yes, textualism and originalism seem to go hand in hand, particularly in the case of the leading textualist and the leading originalist: both terms refer to Justice Scalia.

Consider the Fourteenth Amendment's guarantee of "equal protection." In 1868, when the Amendment was ratified, its "public understanding" unquestionably entailed important civil rights for blacks, like voting, but not the right to attend a desegregated school. Unless a convincing historical argument can be made to the contrary, an originalist is stuck with viewing *Brown v. Board of Education* as wrong. We saw above that Steven Calabresi argues for an originalist, Fourteenth Amendment-based, justification of *Brown,* but Posner's concern about judges reading their own values into old laws (exs. (13) and (14) above) undercuts it. So imagine a change in public opinion: Suppose it becomes broadly accepted that every adult is entitled to a job paying enough to live on, provided, if necessary, by the government. Or that everyone deserves a guaranteed income, regardless of employment status, supplied by the government. Suppose one argument for laws mandating such economic equality is the Fourteenth Amendment's equal protection provision. Would Calabresi agree, saying "Yep, that's what 'equal protection' means, and has always meant"? Would an opponent of government-ensured economic equality argue that Calabresi and supporters of government-guaranteed economic equality were reading into the equal protection clause their own, or popular, values?

Consider next the Eighth Amendment's ban on "cruel and unusual punishment." In 1958 the Supreme Court found unconstitutional, on Eighth Amendment grounds, a statute punishing deserters from the armed forces with loss of citizenship. Chief Justice Earl Warren, writing for the majority, took a decidedly non-originalist stance:

16   [T]he words of the Amendment are not precise, and ... their scope is not static. The Amendment must draw its meaning from the evolving standards of decency that mark the progress of a maturing society.

Trop v. Dulles, 356 U.S. 86 (1958)

Warren's reasoning focused on the cruelty in making a person stateless. Imposition of the penalty brings about

17   the total destruction of the individual's status in organized society. It is a form of punishment more primitive than torture... The punishment strips the citizen of his status in the national and international political community. ... While any one country may accord him some rights ... no country need do so, because he is stateless. Furthermore, his enjoyment of even the limited rights of an alien might be subject to termination at any time ... In short, the expatriate has lost the right to have rights.

This punishment is offensive to cardinal principles for which the Constitution stands. It subjects the individual to a fate of ever-increasing fear and distress. ...He may be subject to banishment, a fate universally decried by civilized people. He is stateless, a condition deplored in the international community of democracies.

Id.

This argument has nothing about the framers' purpose behind the Amendment, nothing about the late eighteenth century world view which was the context of its enactment, and no hint of language-centered analysis. It's all about the unusualness and cruelty of ending a person's citizenship.

A 2010 case shows both sides of the argument. A Florida state court sentenced a minor to life imprisonment with no possibility of parole for some violent attempted robberies. Justice Kennedy, writing for the majority, construed the Amendment in light of present-day standards of cruelty, just as Warren did in 1958:

[18] Life without parole is "the second most severe penalty permitted by law." (cite omitted) ... [L]ife without parole sentences share some characteristics with death sentences ... [T]he sentence alters the offender's life by a forfeiture that is irrevocable. It deprives the convict of the most basic liberties without giving hope of restoration...

...

Life without parole is an especially harsh punishment for a juvenile. Under this sentence a juvenile offender will on average serve more years and a greater percentage of his life in prison than an adult offender. A 16-year-old and a 75-year-old each sentenced to life without parole receive the same punishment in name only.

Graham v. Florida, 560 U.S. 48 (2010)

Kennedy also argued for proportionality between crime and punishment:

[19] The concept of proportionality is central to the Eighth Amendment. Embodied in the Constitution's ban on cruel

and unusual punishments is the "precept of justice that punishment for crime should be graduated and proportioned to [the] offense." (cite omitted)

Id.

In dissent, Justice Thomas, joined by Justice Scalia, took an originalist position:

[20]   [T]he Cruel and Unusual Punishments Clause was originally understood as prohibiting ... methods akin to those that had been considered cruel and unusual at the time the Bill of Rights was adopted (cite omitted).

...

More recently, however, the Court has held that the Clause authorizes it to proscribe not only methods of punishment that qualify as "cruel and unusual," but also any punishment that the Court deems "grossly disproportionate" to the crime committed. ... This latter interpretation is entirely the Court's creation. ... [T]here is virtually no indication that the Cruel and Unusual Punishments Clause originally was understood to require proportionality in sentencing.

Id., Thomas, J., dissenting

And a textualist one: "The Clause does not expressly refer to proportionality or invoke any synonym for that term" (*id.*).

And that's the way it stands. Originalists and non-originalists disagree.

8.3.6 A linguistic take on the issue: sense vs. denotation

Possibly the original *meaning* of vague Constitutional provisions could be preserved, but their *denotation* could be recognized as different from the original public understanding of the denotation. Recall that the denotation of an expression is the set of possible referents for the expression. The denotation of *airplane* is the set of planes, including possible and not-yet existing ones. Nobody knew in 1920 that the denotation of *airplane* included jets. "Meaning" is too broad a term here. Better is German logician Gottlob Frege's term **sense** (German *Sinn*), in contradistinction to **reference** (German *Bedeutung*). Frege (1892) famously distinguished sense and reference by means of the expressions *the morning star* and *the evening star,* both of which denote, and are used to refer to, the planet Venus (their referent, or *bedeutung*) but have different senses. Calabresi's view that the Fourteenth Amendment licensed school desegregation and mixed race and gay marriage can be understood as maintaining the meaning (sense) of *equal protection* but noticing that its denotation includes a lot more than anybody was aware that it did in 1868. Even Scalia countenances such an approach, with respect to the word *speech* in the First Amendment, an analysis which goes beyond textualism:

21   [T]he provision of the First Amendment that forbids abridgement of "the freedom of speech, or of the press" ... does not list the full range of communicative expression. Handwritten letters, for example, are neither speech nor the press. Yet surely there is no doubt they cannot be censored. In this constitutional context, speech and press, the two most common forms of communication, stand as a sort of synechdoche for the whole. This is not strict construction, but it is reasonable construction.

Scalia 1997, 37–38

This comes close to suggesting that speech in the First Amendment really "means" "communication," and did even in 1787, which allows the word to denote, and consequently the First Amendment to protect, not only writing, but also even "symbolic speech" like political flag-burning. Scalia was part of the majority in *Texas v. Johnson,* a 1989 Supreme Court decision finding such flag-burning protected by the First Amendment. One might think that it is a problem for Scalia's position that his only justification for this departure from textualism and originalism is that it is "reasonable," an exercise of just the sort of judicial discretion that Scalia purports to abhor. But the existence of "reasonable" extensions of denotations elsewhere in the construction of Constitutional provisions provides support. For example, under *Miranda v. Arizona*, interrogation includes the "functional equivalent" of direct questioning (*Rhode Island v. Innis*). And government "takings" includes more than straightforward condemnation (as when a government has to level your house to build a freeway), specifically any government policy which removes all possibility of economic gain from the property (*Lucas v. South Carolina Coastal Council*, 505 U.S. 1003 (1992)). In *Lucas*, what had happened was that two years after a man named David Lucas bought South Carolina island property with the intention of building houses on it, South Carolina passed a law barring the construction of any habitable structures on certain erosion-threatened beachfront or near-beach land, resulting in Lucas's investment being reduced to near zero value. In an opinion by Scalia, the Court held that this was equivalent to a "taking" and that Lucas was entitled to compensation. Examples like this of functional equivalency in areas different from speech provide support for extending the sense and denotation of *speech* in the First Amendment to all communication. (See Tiersma 1993 for an extended discussion of treating First Amendment "speech" this way.)

8.4 Syntactic issues

Imagine a statute that reads "Whoever knowingly makes a false statement in any matter within the jurisdiction of any agency of the United States shall be fined not more than $1,000." Now suppose you work for a defense corporation that requires you to complete a company security clearance form asking, among other things, whether you have ever been arrested. You fill out the form and sign it, attesting that the information you have supplied is true and complete. However, you decide to leave out your arrest a few years ago for shoplifting. The charge was minor and the case was dismissed anyway. You figure there's probably be no record of the arrest and it'll just be simpler to leave it out. Wrong! Your omission is discovered, you get fired, and to your shock, you're arrested and charged with violating the statute.

You are clearly in trouble; you did make a false statement on the form. When you tell your story to your lawyer, he asks you whether, when you filled out the form, you knew that the company was going to send your form to the Defense Department. You answer truthfully "No." Your lawyer looks pleased.

At trial, your lawyer points out that the statute is syntactically ambiguous as to the scope of modification of *knowingly.* Like all the fictional sharp lawyers in this book, your lawyer was a linguistics major in college, and he helpfully supplies phrase structure trees showing the ambiguity:

In tree (a), *knowingly* modifies the big verb phrase (VP) *makes a false statement in any matter within the jurisdiction of the United States.* In tree (b), *knowingly* modifies only the smaller VP *makes a false statement,* and the Prepositional Phrase *in any matter...of the United States* has scope over *knowingly makes a false statement.* Your lawyer explains to the jury how to understand tree diagrams. Then he calls you as a witness. You admit that you did knowingly make a false statement, but state emphatically that you had

[22] a.

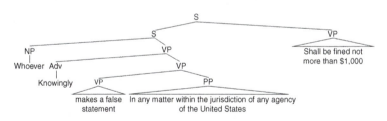

b.

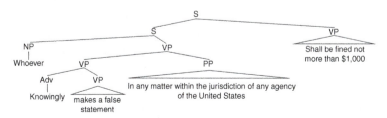

no idea that your employer would send your form to the Defense Department. In other words, you didn't know that your omitting your arrest from the form was "in a matter within the jurisdiction of" a U.S. government department. In his closing statement, your lawyer argues that the rule of lenity means that for the purpose of this case the statute has to be understood with the structure in tree (a). With that structure, *knowingly* modifies the big VP, so with that reading of the statute the prosecution would have had to prove that you knew that you made your false statement in a "matter within the jurisdiction" of the Defense Department. The jury gets it and takes only five minutes to return a verdict of Not Guilty. Your supervisor calls to offer your old job back at double the salary. Mazel tov!

Back to reality. In the actual case that inspired the tale above, a defense contractor employee named Esmail Yermian omitted from his security clearance form his conviction for mail fraud, and the statute under which he was charged was structured differently, reading:

23   Whoever, in any matter within the jurisdiction of any depart-
      ment or agency of the United States, knowingly and willfully
      ... makes any false ... statements ... shall be fined...

                                                      18 U.S.C. § 1001

This is unambiguous. The PP *in any matter...of the United States* modifies *knowingly makes any false statements,* not the other way around:

24

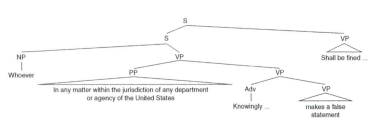

Not surprisingly, Yermian was convicted. On appeal to the Ninth Circuit, miraculously he won. Here's what the court said about the syntax of the statute:

25 We find the language of the statute ambiguous... While ... "knowingly.." clearly provides that specific intent is a crucial element of the offense, neither the grammatical construction nor the punctuation of the statute indicates whether ... "knowingly ..." modifies only the phrase "makes any false... statements" or the broader phrase "in any matter within the jurisdiction of any department or agency of the United States ... makes any false... statements."

U.S. v. Yermian, 708 F.2d 365 (9th Cir. 1983)

To this the presumably astonished prosecutor must have said something like "Are you KIDDING?" The prosecution appealed to the Supreme Court, which reversed the Ninth Circuit and reinstated Yermian's conviction, writing:

26 The jurisdictional language appears in a phrase separate from the prohibited conduct modified by ..."knowingly..." Any natural reading of § 1001, therefore, establishes that ..."knowingly..." modify only the making of "false... statements," and not the predicate circumstance that those statements be made in a matter within the jurisdiction of a federal agency. Once this is clear, there is no basis for requiring proof that the defendant had actual knowledge of federal agency jurisdiction.

U.S. v. Yermian, 468 U.S. 63, 69 (1984)

This is not written the way a linguist would write it, but the Court got it right. What may be surprising is that the Ninth Circuit got it wrong. Also possibly surprising is that the Supreme Court's decision was not unanimous. In fact, it was 5–4, with Justice Rehnquist's dissent joined by Justices Brennan, Stevens, and O'Connor. Rehnquist simply found the language of the statute ambiguous:

27   In my view, it is quite impossible to tell which phrases the
      terms "knowingly and willfully" modify...

                              Id. at 78 (Rehnquist, J., dissenting)

Rehnquist pointed to an earlier version of the statute, which had
the "in any matter within the jurisdiction of..." language after
the verb phrase "makes any false statements," like the made-up
example in our story above, and argued that the revision to the
modern version was just a "housekeeping" change that represented
no Congressional intent to change the substance of the statute.
The focus on Congressional intent rather than plain meaning is of
course the defining characteristic of intentionalism/purposivism.

   Syntax is hard for non-linguists, even very smart ones like
Supreme Court justices. The moral of the syntax story – and there
are other stories, real cases, showing the same failure of very smart
judges to understand grammar – is that a prerequisite to law school
admission should be completion of an undergraduate degree with
a major in linguistics, if not an M.A. or Ph.D. (Ha! Ha! Joke! But
not 100% joke.)

   **You should now read *U.S. v. X-Citement Video*, 513 U.S. 64 (1994),
including Scalia's dissent.**

8.5 Lexical issues

A guy named John Smith (yes, his real name) was interested in buying
cocaine. Smith offered to trade his gun for the drugs. Unfortunately
for Smith, his contact turned out to be an undercover police
informant. He was arrested, tried, and convicted, and in addition
was convicted of violating this punishment-"enhancing" statute:

28   [A]ny person who, during and in relation to any crime of vio-
      lence or drug trafficking crime ... uses or carries a firearm...
      shall, in addition to the punishment provided for such crime
      of violence or drug trafficking crime ... be sentenced to a term
      of imprisonment of not less than 5 years.

                                         18 U.S.C. § 924(c)(1)

The case hinged on what *use* means in the statute. (The indictment didn't mention carrying.) *Use* is one of those semantically vague verbs like *get* that have lots of senses, depending on their **complements** (obligatory following expressions). Just as you can get drunk, get fed, get gas, get lost, get away, get a good grade, get someone to do something, etc., you can, among other things, use a pen, use drugs, use big words, and use people for one's own (selfish or nefarious) purposes (*she's just using him*). In a 1995 paper, law professor Clark Cunningham and linguist Charles Fillmore point out two more characteristics. For full informativeness, *use* needs more than a complement, in the form of an **adjunct** (optional modifier) or from context:

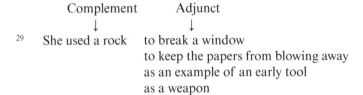

	Complement	Adjunct
	↓	↓
29	She used a rock	to break a window
		to keep the papers from blowing away
		as an example of an early tool
		as a weapon

"She used a rock," with nothing more, is pretty uninformative. This means that a sentence of the form *A used B* is an abbreviation for a longer, semantically complete, sentence *A used B as X* or *A used B to do Y*, in which *X* and *Y* are contextually supplied.

In addition, Cunningham & Fillmore point out, in connection with the words *use a gun* in the statute, that when *use* has as its complement an expression meaning something designed for a specific purpose, like *a gun*, there is a default interpretation: "use for the purpose for which it was designed." That is, without more information in the context or in the utterance itself, that interpretation is strongly implicated. With other complements, like *a rock*, there's no default interpretation. Cunningham & Fillmore write:

30   [I]f we hear somebody say, "I hope I never have to use this gun," we are most likely to assume that the person is speaking about using it for its manufactured purpose... If the phrase "used a gun" was to be used to describe an occasion when a

gun was placed on papers to prevent them from blowing away, a speaker would reasonably assume that the utterance would have been something like, "He used a gun as a paperweight" to signal that the default interpretation was not applicable.

Cunningham & Fillmore 1995, 1179

Cunningham & Fillmore provide the following example to demonstrate the difference between the non-default and the default interpretations:

31   A: This is the gun I use for domestic protection.
     B: Have you ever used it?
     A: No, thank God, I've never had to use it.

Id., 1186

The implication of this semantic analysis for the *Smith* case is clear. Because the statute has no adjunct modifying *use a gun* and there's no context favoring a non-default interpretation, the default interpretation is the most relevant one.

However, when the case got to the Supreme Court, Smith's conviction was upheld. The decision was 6–3, with Justice O'Connor authoring the majority opinion and Justice Scalia the dissent. O'Connor adduced dictionary definitions:

32   Petitioner "used" his MAC-10 in an attempt to obtain drugs by offering to trade it for cocaine.

Webster's defines "to use" as "[t]o convert to one's service" or "to employ." (*Cite omitted.*) Black's Law Dictionary contains a similar definition: "[t]o make use of; to convert to one's service; to employ; to avail oneself of; to utilize; to carry out a purpose or action by means of." (*Cite omitted.*) ...

Petitioner's handling of the MAC-10 in this case falls squarely within those definitions.

Smith v. U.S., 508 U.S. 223 (1993)

Scalia responded that what mattered was *ordinary* meaning:

33 In the search for statutory meaning, we give nontechnical words and phrases their ordinary meaning. ... To use an instrumentality ordinarily means to use it for its intended purpose.

Id., Scalia, J., dissenting

Scalia countered O'Connor's dictionary evidence by arguing like a linguist. He mentioned possibilities of occurrence in different linguistic contexts:

34 When someone asks, "Do you use a cane?," he is not inquiring whether you have your grandfather's silver- handled walking stick on display in the hall; he wants to know whether you walk with a cane. Similarly, to speak of "using a firearm" is to speak of using it for its distinctive purpose, i.e., as a weapon.

...

[T]he objective falsity requirement for a perjury conviction would not be satisfied if a witness answered "no" to a prosecutor's inquiry whether he had ever "used a firearm," even though he had once sold his grandfather's Enfield rifle to a collector.

Id.

Two years later, in *Bailey v. United States,* a case discussed in Chapter 6, the same issue arose, in connection with the same statute. This time the "use" was the presence of a loaded handgun in a bag in the trunk of the defendant's car. The appellate court below had upheld the conviction on a theory of "accessibility and proximity." The Supreme Court reversed. Again, Justice O'Connor wrote the opinion, but this time the decision was unanimous. **You should now read *Bailey v. United States*.** See if you can find evidence from O'Connor's majority opinion that somebody, maybe O'Connor herself, had read Cunningham & Fillmore's paper. Also try to find evidence of influence from Scalia's dissent in *Smith*.

8.6 Conclusion

In this chapter we've explored theories of statutory interpretation – or better, construction – and looked at cases in which the construction of a statute depended on linguistic interpretation of syntax or vocabulary. The prominence given to Justice Scalia's thinking is due to Scalia's linguistic insight and to his linguist-like reasoning. But don't infer that Scalia's opinions are always as linguistically insightful as in the examples cited here. In fact, Scalia's majority opinion in the 2008 case *District of Columbia. v. Heller,* the Second Amendment case, can be criticized for a failure of linguistic insight and even as a radical departure from textualism. Your author has so argued (Kaplan 2012).

The argument between textualism and originalism on the one hand and purposivism and anti-originalism on the other is likely to continue, but that should not blind us to the fact that generally the Constitution and statutes work pretty well. The cases that get to the Supreme Court are not only the hard ones but also the rare ones.

Chapter 9

Trademarks

9.0 Introduction

Suppose you're an entrepreneur with something you want to market. You come up with a clever name for it. It might be a word or short phrase, or a made-up sequence of sounds. You might choose an expression that already has another meaning, or evokes one. Let's say your product is a sponge. You decide to name it "Squoze," a nonstandard past tense of *squeeze*. "Squoze" will appear on your product or your product's packaging and in your advertising. You can register it as a trademark with the U.S. Patent and Trademark Office (USPTO). Doing this will deter other entrepreneurs who want to use the same or a similar term; when they try to register their would-be trademark, yours will show up, and they'll try a different trademark. If they don't, you'll be able to challenge their attempted registration.

Registration helps protect your product's, and your company's, reputation, by making it harder for a competitor to use the same or a similar **mark** (short for *trademark*), and therefore helps protect your product and company from being confused with another product (maybe lousy) or company (maybe sleazy). If Squoze sponges are good, and a competitor markets a lousy sponge called Squoze Junior, consumers might mistake the latter for the former, to their, and your, detriment.

Having a registered trademark is useful because it creates the legal presumption that your trademark is valid. It creates a warning to the world that you claim the exclusive right to use the mark, and if you have to defend your mark in court, places the burden of proof on the party opposing your mark.

Not just names can be trademarked. Phrases, for example slogans, can be too (example: Capital One Financial's "What's in your wallet?"), as well as logos, images, and physical forms like McDonald's golden arches.

9.0.1 A hierarchy of trademark strength

Trademark law divides trademarks into four categories with different levels of "strength." In this context *strength* means "distinctiveness," specifically distinctness of *denotation* – the set of possible referents, that is, your products, or your company (in which case the set of possible referents has just one member). The concept of distinctness of denotation can be informally extended to non-name trademarks. Just as *Apple* denotes Apple (and Apple computers), Capital One's slogan stands for Capital One, and McDonald's arches stand for McDonalds, to the extent that the slogan and the arches consistently evoke those entities in people's minds.

Here are the categories in rank order, strongest to weakest:

- **Fanciful**: invented expressions like *Google, Xerox,* and *Kodak.*
- **Arbitrary**: existing expressions with no natural semantic relation to the product or service: *Apple* (computers), *Ivory* (soap), *Three Twins* (ice cream).
- **Suggestive**: expressions with a weak natural semantic connection to the product or service, requiring some sort of mental leap: *Greyhound* (bus line), *Kitchen Aid* (kitchen appliances), *Netflix* (online movies).
- **Descriptive**: expressions with an obvious natural semantic connection to the kind of product or service, or an attribute of it, with no imaginative leap required: *Oatnut* (bread containing oats and nuts), *1-888-M-A-T-R-E-S-S* (a company selling mattresses over the phone), *Chocolate Fudge* (chocolate fudge flavored diet soda).

Descriptive trademarks are often described as "mere," and usually the USPTO won't permit their registration. However, descriptive trademarks can, through market success, acquire distinctiveness, and thereby trademark protection, by becoming associated with a particular company or product line, in the minds of lots of members of a relevant community. When this happens, the expression is said to have acquired **secondary meaning**. Now it's a name. A frequently mentioned example is Sharp televisions. The trademark *Sharp* is used to refer to the Sharp company. Because a trademark identifies products as well as their maker, the trademark *Sharp* also denotes all Sharp televisions. To the extent that a trademark is widely known and used as a name, that secondary meaning can eclipse the original meaning. The word *Sharp*, when used refer to TVs or a company, loses much of its original sense. The reason is that names don't have senses, just referents.

When trademarks are used to refer to products, grammatically they're common nouns, occurring after determiners (*a Tesla*) and being pluralizable (*two Teslas*). When used to refer to a company, a trademark is a proper noun (*Tesla is an interesting company*).

The distinction between "suggestive" and "descriptive" trademarks is fuzzy. This fuzziness gives rise to trademark battles in court, since suggestive trademarks can get protection but descriptive ones generally can't. In principle, descriptive trademarks have a direct relationship to the nature of the good or service they denote, whereas suggestive trademarks require an imaginative leap to get there. Examples: Holiday Inn (hotels), All Bran (cereal), Bank of America (bank) are descriptive. L'eggs (pantyhose) and Glass Doctor (window repair) are suggestive.

Also in the mix are **generic** trademarks, which get no legal protection. "Generic" in trademark law means something different from what it means in linguistics. In linguistics, generic sentences describe typical characteristics of examples of types. *The cheetah is capable of astounding speed* is a generic sentence because it's true generally of cheetahs (not universally true; it's not made false by the discovery of a poky cheetah). But in trademark law, "generic" is the term for expressions like verbs, adjectives, and, especially, common nouns, that is, expressions which have **senses** (roughly, the kind of meanings dictionary definitions clue one into) in addition to denotations. Generic expressions thus are basically contentful expressions of all kinds except proper nouns, i.e., names. ("Contentful" rules out forms with grammatical function, like determiners.) Generics denote *kinds* of things. *Cookie, wine,* and *quick* denote kinds of things (cookies, wine, and quick things) and are therefore generic terms, in the terminology of trademark law.

Sponge is generic because it denotes a kind of thing, sponges. If you try to register a trademark like "Sponge" for your new sponge product, the USPTO won't let you. If you want, you can use it as your trademark, but you'll have a hard time defending it if somebody else starts using it, or something similar, for the same or a similar sort of product.

Obviously, the categories of "generic" and "descriptive" expressions overlap. The word *sharp* describes a property of a good TV, so the trademark "Sharp" is descriptive, but it's also generic, because it denotes a kind of thing, namely things that are sharp. There's a tendency in the law world to restrict the application of *generic* to unmodified common nouns (like *sponge*) and to apply *descriptive* to verbs, adjectives, adverbs, and modified common nouns. Under trademark law, *Sponge* is probably generic, whereas *Squeezy Sponge* and *Squeezy* – and *Sharp* – are probably descriptive.

Where "generic" and "descriptive" *don't* overlap is **genericized** fanciful trademarks, made-up expressions which as a result of market success have become generic. Well-known examples include *aspirin, escalator, trampoline,* and *thermos,* all of which began life as fanciful trademarks. Such expressions are not descriptive; since they're made-up words, specifically invented to be names, they don't describe anything. They just denote.

The only tricky descriptive issue is this. Trademarks have a double nature, as proper noun used to refer to a company, and as a common noun denoting the company's products. What distinguishes the latter from generic expressions is their semantic tie to their parent company, the association in the minds of most members of the relevant public between product and source. So, *a Tesla* is associated with *Tesla,* the company, but *thermos,* the genericized common noun, has lost its semantic connection to the American Thermos company.

9.1 Similarities in sound and meaning

In the 1990s a trademark battle erupted between two corporations selling lines of packaged food products, including microwavable cup items, with the names "Healthy Choice" and "Health Selections." Each side hired an expert linguist. One was Roger Shuy, whose account in Shuy 2002 is the basis for the summary below. Shuy does not identify the other linguist. With two similar names and products, it's easy to imagine either one of the corporate parents suing the other. In fact, it was the seller of "Healthy Choice," ConAgra, that sued the seller of "Health Selections," Hormel. ConAgra wanted to convince the court that the trademarks were similar enough to cause consumer confusion, with Hormel taking the opposite position. Shuy was hired as an expert by Hormel.

Three linguistic levels were involved: phonology, grammar, and semantics.

On the question of phonological similarity, ConAgra's linguist argued that the sound similarity between *healthy* and *health* outweighed the difference between the marks' second words *choice* and *selections,* partly on the grounds that initial parts of expressions matter more for phonological distinctions than later parts. The linguist noted that word-final consonant deletion in some dialects – as with /r/ in words like *car* – occurs with little if any loss of meaning distinctions. If you hear a Bostonian suggest taking the [kʰaa], you'll understand "car." In contrast, initial sound segments, like the /r/ in *red,* tend not to be lost. No /r/-deleter says [ɛd] for *red.* Shuy, Hormel's linguist, countered that initial parts of words can be reduced, as in *'member* for *remember* and *'cause* for *because,* with no loss of meaning. ConAgra's linguist also argued that nicknames tend to preserve the first part of names, reducing later parts, as in *Mike* for *Michael* and *Al* for *Alan.* Shuy countered with *Tina* for *Christina* and *Gene* for *Eugene.* Neither linguist seems to have mentioned that the stressed syllable in names tends to be the one that is preserved in nicknames: *Ginny* for *Virginia, Liz* for *Elizabeth, Trish* for *Patricia.* (I said "tends to"; there are counterexamples like *Beth* and *Pat.*) ConAgra's linguist argued that in word sequences, like *first choice,* the initial consonant of the second word is never lost, in contrast with the final consonant of the first word, which is often deleted. Shuy countered with examples of sounds being added to the beginnings of words in some dialects: *a-* in "acoming" and similar forms and /h/ in *h'aint,* casting doubt on the significance of initial position. Shuy made an additional phonological argument, discounting first vs. later position and simply counting the number of differences between the phonemic makeup of the whole two expressions. Of the thirteen phonemes in *health selections,* eight are different from those in *healthy choice.*

With respect to grammar, both linguists agreed that both marks were proper nouns and full noun phrases (NPs), and singular in number, despite the plural *-s* on *selections:* you can say "Health Selections *is* good," not "...*are*..." Both linguists also agreed that as proper nouns, neither mark permitted modifiers (you can't say **Very Healthy Choice is good.*). The ConAgra linguist inferred from these identical properties that the internal grammatical differences – that *health* is a noun, *healthy* an adjective, and *selections* is plural, *choice* singular – don't matter. Shuy disagreed, arguing that the plural *selections* was significant, citing other full NP brand names with plurals, like *Yellow Pages,* and asking rhetorically whether anyone could really believe there was only one yellow page. Shuy also observed that internally the only similarity between the two marks' forms was their shared morpheme *health.*

As for meaning, there are two levels to the meaning of proper noun phrases like these marks: (i) the referential nature of the meaning of proper nouns, and (ii) the fact that these names are composed of common nouns and adjectives, with their meanings. Non-trademark analogs might be "Beantown" for Boston and "Down Under" for Australia and New Zealand. The ConAgra linguist noted the referential nature of proper nouns but also pointed to the semantic similarities between the two marks' component words. The gist of both marks, this linguist claimed, was "items the selection of which can be expected to result in some sort of health benefit" (Shuy 2002: 74). Shuy responded that exact synonymy is nonexistent or rare, and looked more closely at the meanings of the component words. His analysis included a focus on meaning differences between *choice* and *selections*. He observed that *choice* involves identity between the person making the choice and the beneficiary of the choice, whereas *selection* is open to the possibility that someone else makes the decision, as can be seen in a minimal pair: *This choice is yours* (the addressee makes the pick) vs. *This selection is yours* (someone other than the addressee made the pick). He underscored this argument with a topical example: "A woman should have a choice (not selection) when it comes to deciding what to do with her body" (*Id*: 78). Summing up the semantic disagreement between the linguists, the ConAgra linguist opined that the "gists" of the two marks were the same, Shuy that the gist of *Healthy Choice* was "You can make a healthy choice" while the gist of *Health Selections* was "A number of products have been selected for you."

This tale of warring linguists should not obscure the truth, which is that these two trademarks are *somewhat* similar. Linguistic reality is sometimes scalar rather than binary, an example being word class classification. There are more and less "nouny" nouns, with concrete common nouns like *desk* at one end of the scale and abstract nouns (*honesty*), event nouns (*sneeze*), and proper nouns (*Antarctica*) lacking one or more of nouns' prototypical properties (denoting entities, being pluralizable, being able to occur immediately after determiners). The less "nouny" ones are more nouny than they are "verby" or "adjectivy," though, so under a binary view of reality they're nouns. But a binary view of reality is not as accurate as a more nuanced gradient one.

But courts have to make binary decisions: guilty or not guilty, liable or not. In the case at hand, the legal question was whether Hormel had infringed ConAgra's trademark by using a mark that was likely to confuse consumers into believing that Hormel's products were ConAgra's. The linguistic arguments were relevant to that question, but not the whole story. Other arguments were made by the two sides, including arguments about the look of the trademarks. On the linguistic evidence, the judge (it was a bench trial; no jury) agreed with Shuy that the sounds of the two marks were significantly different but with the ConAgra linguist that their meanings were very similar. The judge cited other cases holding that near-identity of meaning did not guarantee confusion. Other factors (such as the marks' appearance) could play a role. The judge decided that the likelihood of confusion was small, thereby awarding the victory to Hormel. ConAgra appealed but lost (*ConAgra v. Hormel,* 990 F.2d 368 (1993). Anticlimactic epilogue to the saga: even though victorious, Hormel decided to drop its "Health Selections" line and to use instead its trademark "Dinty Moore" for its microwavable cup items.

9.2 Marketplace power, secondary meaning, and genericity: the case of Mc-(Donald's)

In 1987, a hotel corporation, Quality Inns, decided to open a line of inexpensive motels that they planned to name "McSleep." The McDonald's corporation objected, and the battle was on. The issue was the meaning of the form *Mc-*. McDonald's' central claim was that Quality Inns' choice of the trademark "McSleep" was an effort to benefit from McDonald's' high reputation as a seller of inexpensive, basic products that were consistent in nature and quality. According to McDonald's, the similarity in form and meaning would create a likelihood of public belief that McSleep motels were associated with McDonald's, even though motels and burgers 'n' fries are different sorts of things.

Again, each side hired a linguist as expert, and again one of them was Roger Shuy. Again, Shuy published an account of his work in this case, which is the basis for what you'll read here, and again he did not identify the opposing linguist (Shuy 2002, *op. cit..*).

McDonald's' advertising had promoted the generalizing of the *Mc-* prefix to McDonald's items like "McFries" and "McShakes," and in doing so had sent their mascot Ronald McDonald out to public events where he taught children to add the prefix to other words ("McBest"). At trial a McDonald's executive testified that the aim of this advertising campaign was to foster the development of a "McLanguage" associated with McDonald's.

The campaign may have succeeded too well. The Quality Inns linguist found numerous new words containing *Mc-*, none of them connected to McDonald's or to the fast food industry: *McBook, McCinema, McHospital, McNews, McOilchange, McSurgery, McTax, McSweater, McPrisons, McPaper* (used to refer to USA Today), *McLaw* (in a law journal article about cheap, easily accessible legal services), and lots of others. Such words, the linguist argued, constituted evidence that the *Mc-* prefix had become genericized to mean "inexpensive, basic, convenient, predictably same, lowbrow," even if for many people that meaning included "McDonald's-like," as a metaphorical extension. And, the linguist argued, linguistic context ruled out any non-metaphorical (i.e., genuine) connection to the McDonald's corporation. No one reading an article about newspapers containing a reference to USA Today as a McPaper would infer that USA Today was owned by the McDonald's corporation.

The semantic question was therefore to what extent *Mc-* had become freed from its association with McDonald's. As in the Healthy Choice – Health Selections case, the true answer was probably "somewhat." And as in that case, the judge (again it was a bench trial) had to decide on a winner and a loser. The judge found for McDonald's. According to the judge, *Mc-* had NOT become generic, and confusion WAS likely between McSleep motels and McDonald's, so McDonald's' trademark was protected and the corporate parent of McSleep motels would not be permitted to use that name. The judge thus found that secondary meaning had prevailed over genericity, due to McDonald's' huge advertising efforts and massive presence in the culture.

After this case was decided, McDonald's introduced new *Mc-* words like *McSpace Station, McFamily, McTravel, McBunny,* and others. Writing about the case, Shuy commented "It appears that this huge company has a monopoly on the prefix 'Mc-,' and that the public domain will have to get along the best we can without using it in its generic meaning" (2002:109). Shuy's comment is too pessimistic. All that the decision in the case means is that businesses can't use *Mc-* as, or in, a trademark. "We" in the "public domain" can use it all we want, to mean "basic, predictable, cheap, lowbrow," with or without a metaphorical association with McDonald's.

You should now read Playtex Products, Inc., *Plaintiff-appellant,* *v.* *Georgia-pacific* *Corporation* *and* *Fort* *James* *Operating* *Corporation, Defendants-appellees,* **390 F.3d 158 (2d Cir. 2004)**

9.3 Fighting about genericness: *Google*

Everybody, or at least everybody who reads this book, knows how to google. Almost all the time when googlers google, they use the search engine Google. There are other search engines (Bing, Yahoo), but they have tiny market shares. Recall that as *generic* is used in law discourse, generic expressions denote kinds of entities, rather than being proper nouns used to refer to individual entities. A panel of the Ninth Circuit, the appellate court that finally decided the case you're about to read about, described the distinction as a "who are you / what are you" test: "If the relevant public primarily understands a mark as describing 'who' a particular good or service is, or where it comes from, then the mark is still valid. But if the relevant public primarily understands a mark as describing 'what' the particular good or service is, then the mark has become generic." (*Elliott v. Google, Inc.,* 860 F.3d 1151 (9th Cir. 2017).)

This formulation presupposes that the expression in question is a noun or noun phrase, and the "test" the court identified can be translated into linguistics-talk as whether the trademark is used and understood mainly as a common noun (with no semantic connection to a parent company) or as a proper noun (a name). *Google* is also a verb. Does *google* (the verb) mean, to those who understand or use it, "use Google to search the internet," a so-called *discriminate* sense, in the terminology of the trial court, or just "search the internet," an *indiscriminate* sense? (In linguistics-talk, we could distinguish *specific* from *nonspecific* or *referential* from *nonreferential.*) If it means the former, this is evidence that Google, the company, has a valid trademark; if it means the latter, this is evidence (but not proof: stay tuned) that the Google trademark has become genericized. In the ghoulish parlance of trademark law, as the ironic price of success, it may have become a victim of **genericide**. (Interesting word: Based on *fratricide, regicide,* and *suicide,* it seems like it should mean killing the generic, but it means killing the trademark.)

As mentioned above, genericized former trademarks include *aspirin, escalator, trampoline,* and *thermos.* Each of these began life as a trademark, and each was held by a court to have been genericized. Then there are Kleenex and Xerox (and others), with still-valid trademarks, but whose trademarks have also become ordinary nouns (and verbs, in the case of *xerox*). If a company called Kleano were to sell its products, say wet wipes, or even – maybe – tissues, as Kleano Kleenex, it might get away with it. Butters 2012 calls *Kleenex* and *Xerox* "pseudogenerics." Butters suggests that *Google* fits into this category, but actually it may be "less pseudogeneric," and in fact less generic, than *kleenex* and *xerox. Kleenex* and *xerox* denote things marketed by a range of different corporations. Other tissue brands include Puffs, Scotties, Nice 'n' Soft, and store brands, all of whose products are often referred to as *kleenex.* Besides Xerox, successful photocopier companies include Canon, Konica Minolta, and Ricoh, all of whose machines are often called *xerox machines;* and the verb *to xerox* is commonly used to mean "to photocopy," regardless of what brand of copy machine is used. In contrast, the noun *Google*'s denotation seems to be exclusively the Google search engine.

In 2014 two entrepreneurs named David Elliott and Chris Gillespie sued in federal court seeking a declaratory judgment that *google* was generic. Google countersued for trademark infringement. Both sides hired linguists as experts. Unlike Roger Shuy (see above), these linguists have not gone public with their analyses by publishing articles about the case or (as far as I know) by giving talks about it. For that reason they will not be identified here. The primary linguistic argument made in support of Elliott and Gillespie was that because *google* had become a verb, it was generic. As a verb, it was grammatically able to accept derivational affixes, as in this naturally occurring example cited in a linguist's report:

1   We become experts in the syntax and constraints of Google, Yahoo, Altavista, and so on. We become "googleologists."

In this example the root verb *google* can only stand for searching the internet generally, not searching the internet by using Google. While not the whole story (again, stay tuned), this example is evidence of genericization. Other naturally occurring data offered to support a conclusion of genericization include these:

2   The American Dialect Society's (ADS) choice of *google* as its Word of the Decade 2000–2009, with the ADS's definition:

   Google: Verb meaning "to search the Internet." Generic form of the trademarked "Google," the world's dominant Internet search engine.

3   Headline and sidebar from an article from the Pew Research Center

   Teachers Say that for Students Today Research = Googling.

   94%
   Teachers overwhelmingly say
   Google or other search engines tops
   list of sources their students use for
   research.

   www.pewresearch.org/fact-tank/2012/12/06/teachers-say-that-for-students-today- research-googling/

4   Avril kicks out husband "We challenge any Juiceheads to actually know what Avril Lavigne is up to these days without Googling it on Bing."

St Petersburg Times, Sept. 18, 2009

Examples like (1)-(4) are rare. Much more common are uses of the verb *google* in which it is impossible to tell the speaker's intention: to mean "search the internet using Google," or simply "search the internet":

5   Should I let my date know I googled her?

Hello!
so on Friday I am meeting with the girl next door. We've been neighbors for 2 years or so - but barely had any contact apart from occasionally meeting her in the stairwell. I asked her out and she said why not (yes!:D). Anyway I wonder if I can bring up that I googled her? Or could this in any way be seen as creepy?

www.reddit.com/r/AskWomen/comments/2gnl7v/should_i_
let_my_date_know_i_googled_her/

A third possible reading for examples like (5), suggested by Google's linguist, is a **representative** use. In a representative use, an expression identifies a type, not like generics do, but through synecdoche – "part for the whole" – so the expression implicates the type without actually denoting it. Confused? An example may help. Here's one from the same linguist: The reminder at the end of daylight savings time every fall to "set your clock back" applies not just to clocks, but also to watches, phones, and maybe sprinkler systems for lawns or gardens, but no one would think that such a use means that *clock* denotes time-measuring devices of any sort. In the same way, it's possible that examples like (5) are representative rather than generic. Because Google is so commonly used, the speaker uses *google* to convey "do an internet search" by using a word with a more limited denotation.

Google's linguist speculated about why *google* became so popular a verb, whereas, in contrast, trademarks like Excel, Word, and Powerpoint didn't. Nobody says "I'll Excel these numbers for you." According to this linguist, while the answer is complex, with several factors interacting, one important factor is just cultural accident. In the early 2000s, soon after Google was introduced to the marketplace, it was used mainly by young internet-savvy professionals to check out potential new boyfriends or girlfriends. From a 2001 New York Times story:

6   According to dating experts, it is increasingly common for people to perform Web searches on their prospective mates. A search engine that is often used for this activity is called Google (www.google.com), which has spawned a new verb, to google, as uttered in sentences like, "I met this woman last night at a party and I came right home and googled her."

"The Dating Game, Deleted," The New York Times,
March 11, 2001

The popularity of this use of Google helped give Google the social significance of being really cool. In other words, one factor contributing to the verbing of the trademark was its partly accidental success in popular fashion.

The defining statute for trademark law is the Lanham Act, passed in 1946, and named for Texas Congressman Fritz Lanham, a leading proponent of federal trademark protection. Besides explaining how to register a trademark and laying out how trademark owners can get federal protection for their trademark, it provides that a trademark may be cancelled if it has become "the generic name for the goods or services…for which it is registered" (15 U.S.C § 1064(3). Mentions of *name(s) for … goods or services* recur in the Act. A strict – textualist – reading of this expression therefore limits genericide to nouns or NPs. The "who vs. what" test mentioned above has the same limitation. The battle between textualism and purposivism seems not to have been mentioned in this case, but both the trial court and the appellate court did cite this language against Elliott and Gillespie's argument that the verb *google* meaning "search the internet, regardless of search engine" was proof of genericization. Both courts held that even if the VERB *google* meant that to the relevant public, this was not proof of genericization. What would constitute proof of genericization would be predominant public use of the NOUN *google* to mean "internet search engine," with a denotation including other search engines besides Google. There is no such use, at least at the time of this writing (early 2019): no one calls Google, or Yahoo, or Bing, *a google.*

The Lanham Act's drafters can be criticized for failing to recognize in the words of the Act the fact that English permits nouns to become verbs fairly freely (examples: *to salt, to water, to access, to contact*). A purposivist might argue that the purpose behind the act would be served by going beyond the noun-or-NP presupposition and accepting the common use of the verb *google* as evidence (while not necessarily proof) of genericity.

There are plenty of examples of trademark battles over genericization-or-not in which it's only noun uses that occur (*thermos, escalator, trampoline,* e.g.). Relevant evidence can be purely linguistic, for instance findings of widespread use in the relevant speech community of a trademark as a common noun with a denotation considerably wider than that of the trademark: *a thermos, a kleenex.* Or it can be surveys. The two main types of surveys used in trademark cases are **Thermos** surveys and **Teflon** surveys, named after trademarks whose genericity was tested in cases (*American Thermos Prod. Co. v. Aladdin Industries, Inc.* (1962) for *thermos* and *E.I. Du Pont de Nemours & Co. v. Yoshida Int'l, Inc.* (1975) for *Teflon*). In a Thermos survey, subjects are asked open-ended questions, including one or more about how they would request a certain product (for example, from a store clerk) or how they would describe it. In a Teflon survey, after being shown the difference between a "brand name" and a "common name," with examples (like *Chevrolet* and *automobile*), subjects are presented with a short list of words or phrases, with no context provided, and asked to classify each as a "brand name" or as a "common name" (with some variation in wording, for example, instead of "brand name," some surveys use "trade name"). In the Google case, Google used a Teflon survey. Subjects were asked over the phone to apply the distinction between brand names and "common names" to *browser, website, Amazon, Yahoo,* and *Google,* in connection with internet searches. *Google* was identified as a brand name by over 93% of respondents. *Amazon* and *Yahoo* also got extremely high scores for brand name. Elliott and Gillespie used a modified Thermos survey, which subjects were asked "If you were going to ask a friend to search for something on the Internet, what word or phrase would you use to tell him/her what you want him/her to do?" – a question designed to elicit a verb answer. Responses from a little over half the subjects contained the word *google.*

The surveys used by the respective sides seem to have been chosen to produce the desired results. Google's Teflon survey gave subjects a binary choice, "brand name" or "common name." Answers of "both" were counted, but subjects were not told that "both" was a possible answer. This design obscures the possibility that the word *google* is recognized as a brand name while also functioning generically. Possible examples: Kleenex, Xerox, Scotch tape, Jacuzzi, all valid trademarks with widespread generic common noun uses. It was pointed out above that truth can be scalar, but courts have to decide in a binary fashion. Google's Teflon survey also precluded answers showing verb uses. Elliott and Gillespie's modified Thermos survey – modified by using a question eliciting verb uses – precluded answers about noun use. Noun use evidence would be less than helpful to Elliott and Gillespie since there's no generic common noun *google* (*Bing is a google is pretty bad). Contrast other trademarks: Kleenex, Scotch tape, Jacuzzi, Band-Aid, Crock-Pot, Frisbee, Hula Hoop, and others, for which generic common nouns exist (*a kleenex, a frisbee*).

Elliott and Gillespie lost at trial and on appeal. And they lost convincingly, by **summary judgment** at trial, a result which was upheld on appeal. Summary judgment is warranted when a court finds that there is no triable issue of fact. When a party moves for summary judgment, the judge assumes as true the factual claims made by the other side. If, under that assumption, the party seeking summary judgment still has the winning argument – the other side's facts and the law cannot possibly overcome the first side's position – there's nothing for a trial to find out, and the motion for summary judgment is granted. There's no trial; the case is over. In the Google case, both sides moved for summary judgment. Google's motion prevailed because Elliott and Gillespie's main factual claim – that the verb *google* was the most common way for internet users to express the meaning "search the internet (regardless of search engine)" – was irrelevant. The reason it was irrelevant was that, under the Lanham Act, genericide could be found only from very widespread NOUN use of a generic. Elliott and Gillespie's motion failed for the same reason.

After losing at trial and on appeal, Elliott and Gillespie appealed to the Supreme Court, but the Court declined to hear the appeal (138 S.Ct. 362 (2017)), leaving the Ninth Circuit decision in place.

The trial court in the Google case made one more point. A conclusion of genericness is supported if the trademark expression is the default way of referring to the product or service in question, and, conversely, if there are equally accurate and easy-to-use ways of referring to it, genericness is not supported:

[7]   If competitors can accurately describe their products or services without using the mark in question, it suggests the mark is not generic. ... In this case, "internet search engines" is the short and simple descriptive term for the genus to which the Google search engine belongs. It is undisputed that competing search engine providers Yahoo! and Microsoft Bing routinely distinguish their search engine services from Google's search engine service in press releases and advertising campaigns. ... Thus, there is no evidence of competitors' usage capable of supporting the inference that the word google has become the common descriptive term for the category of services to which the Google search engine belongs: internet search engines.

Elliott v. Google, 45 F.Supp.3d 1156 (2014)

It may be debatable whether *internet search engine* is short and simple, but it's undeniable that the noun *google* is not "the common descriptive term" for internet search engines. And under the noun-centric strict reading of the governing statute, the verb *google* is irrelevant.

The reality may be that the verb *to google* is, in effect, generic, that is, used mainly with no reference to Google, meaning just "to search the internet." It's also possible that that verb mainly means "to search the internet using Google." Even in the first scenario, under the law as strictly construed, the noun *Google* is a proper noun used to refer to the Google internet search engine which is protectable as a valid trademark.

9.4 Conclusion

We've seen how linguistic properties of trademarks can be used to distinguish between, or make precise the similarities of, partly similar marks: phonology, morphology, syntax, and semantics in the Healthy Choice – Health Selections case, and the semantics of a bound morpheme in the *Mc-* case. We've also looked at the phenomenon of genericization, in our discussion of the Google case, where grammatical evidence – *google* as a verb – was held irrelevant because a textualist reading of the governing statute restricted genericization to nouns. A purposivist or public policy-based reading might have led to a different outcome, but not necessarily. The meaning of the verb *google* might still be, predominantly in the relevant community, "use the search engine Google."

Besides the (very basic) rudiments of trademark law, your takeaway from this chapter should be appreciation of how linguistic findings can be relevant to resolving trademark disputes.

Chapter 10

Conclusion

Law is a vast field, both in its breadth and in the number of its practitioners. Linguistics may be smaller in breadth and is way smaller in its number of practitioners. Based on reports from state bar associations and licensing agencies, there are over 1.3 million active lawyers in the U.S. (www.statista.com/statistics/740222/number-of-lawyers-us/). There are only about 4,000 members of the Linguistic Society of America, the leading professional organization for linguists. Linguistics is also a field whose subject matter is not part of most people's store of knowledge. Other sciences do better; most people have some idea of what geology, chemistry, and biology are about. Most linguistics students and professional linguists have had the experience of telling someone that they do linguistics and receiving in response a brief silence, perhaps followed by a guess as to what linguistics involves ("Oh, you study language history?"), a question about how many languages the linguist speaks, or a lame manifestation of linguistic insecurity ("Ooh, I'd better watch what I say!"). All this works together to make it hard for linguistics to help law. I sometimes think of law as a giant ship proceeding ponderously through waves, difficult to turn, and linguistics as a solitary little tugboat trying to nudge the giant ship, a little, toward a better direction. Nonetheless, there's hope. Linguistics is becoming somewhat more familiar to the public, and also to legal practitioners on that giant ship, as linguists continue to be asked to serve as experts in legal cases. We are far from the "guaranteed full employment for linguists" situation that we'd prefer, but there's progress.

What you've encountered in the previous chapters is about the intersection of law and linguistics, touching only some areas of law. Linguists sometimes expect law to be mostly an application of linguistics. Nope. The understanding of most crimes and torts is not enhanced by linguistics. Most property law isn't either (though at least one bit is – check out, if you're curious and well caffeinated, **vested vs. contingent remainders**, and see if you can see how syntax can distinguish them). Remedies – legal theory about what recompense is right for harm caused – isn't helped by linguistics either. Law governing elections, government structure, business, federalism (the relations between states and the federal government), and civil procedure all get along fine without linguistics. Where linguistics is relevant is in areas of law where communication is intrinsic to the nature of the phenomenon in question: legislation, contract formation and interpretation, communication between law enforcement personnel and criminal suspects, out-of-court communication by suspects, and trademark law. And wills, trusts, threats, and bribery – topics precluded by space limitations from discussion in this book.

Not only is linguistics irrelevant to most areas of law, but in the areas where it IS relevant, law folks don't assume its relevance, though sometimes they see it when it is pointed out. Example: A contract is sometimes defined in law discourse as "an agreement the law will enforce," which raises the question "how are we to know which agreements the law will enforce?" That useless legal definition recurs in contract casebooks and other publications for law students. A contract is a pair of mutual promises, each conditioned on the other. In the first few weeks of my law school adventure, in Contracts class one evening, the professor lectured at length about these mutual conditioned promises without ever mentioning what was obvious to me, namely, that contract formation is a speech act. Losing self-control, I blurted that out: "It's a speech act!" The professor, no dummy, looked bemused and then said, almost to himself, "Why didn't I see that?"

We saw, in Chapters 2, 3, and 4, the usefulness of speech act theory and Gricean implicature to understand communications between police officers and detainees and suspects, and to understand how the law sometimes gets things wrong, for example in how implicature – non-literal, non-explicit communication – is treated in different contexts. Courts allow adoptive admissions in as evidence without recognizing how silence can represent other things than admissions, an instance of, in effect, extrapolating Gricean understanding of communication too far. On the other hand, subtleties of ordinary communication go ignored in interpreting speech by suspects that has been surreptitiously recorded. ("Yeah" doesn't always mean "I agree.") Non-literal behavior in the context of waiving rights is fine, the legal system says, as it is in consenting to searches or other police activity, but arrestees have to be absolutely literal, explicit, and unambiguous in order to request an attorney or to invoke their Constitutional right to silence, and normal ways of requesting – via indirect speech acts – just don't count.

Chapter 5 looked at perjury, defamation, solicitation, and conspiracy, examples of offenses that are intrinsically linguistic in nature, and the understanding of which requires speech act theory and Gricean implicature.

In Chapter 6 we looked at the question of whether there is a "language" of the law, and concluded "Not really," but nonetheless legal discourse, and its interpretation, have unique linguistic properties, and some areas of law, like ambiguous statutes, can be significantly assisted by linguistic analysis.

Chapter 7 introduced you to contract law, most importantly how contracts can be understood as mutual conditioned promises.

In Chapter 8 you met legal theories of statutory construction, contrasting textualism with purposivism or "doing justice-ism," and originalism with non-originalism in statutory and constitutional construction, areas where political theory matters. Do we care more about doing justice – in a particular case, or on a grand scale - or about maintaining the stability and predictability of law? How important is the separation of powers between the legislative and judicial branches, and if the answer is "very important," from which branch is the greater danger of unchecked majoritarianism? We then looked at some ways linguistics can elucidate statutory and constitutional construction, in instances of vagueness and ambiguity. Both syntax and lexical semantics contribute.

Finally, in Chapter 9, you encountered the basics of trademark law, and we looked in detail at three cases in which linguistic analysis played a significant role.

What about the future, for linguistics-and-law, and for the intended and hoped-for audience of this book, that is, people with interest in linguistics, who also have an interest in law? For the small (though obviously incredibly fascinating) field of linguistics-and-law, it was suggested above that guarded optimism is in order about continued growth in the law world's recognition and acceptance of how linguistics can contribute to it. However, law is not a science, so there won't be a scientific breakthrough that will suddenly bring lots more linguistics, and linguists, into helping law. Exception: Possible scientific advances in phonetics could lead to greater accuracy and reliability in speaker identification – an area of law that *is* science-based, or, at least, relies on science.

For you, assuming you are one of the hoped-for set of readers identified above, by far the best route to involvement in linguistic-and-law is to pursue graduate study in linguistics. With a Ph.D. in linguistics you'll have what you need, especially if your studies include lots of pragmatics and semantics. Legal training would be a bonus, but as you have seen, linguistics-and-law is application of linguistics to legal matters, not the application of legal theory to language. Most individuals who work in linguistics-and-law have no formal legal training but lots of linguistic training and experience. Most are linguistics Ph.D.s with posts in linguistics departments. I know of one leading figure with the opposite profile, a law degree and a faculty position in a law school, and no formal training in linguistics. But that's rare.

Another route is law school and a career in law. There is literally no better training for law than linguistics. Linguists and law folks engage in, and love, logical argumentation, and likewise do and enjoy similar sorts of fine-grained analyses of language. Some say they share the same rare genetic quirk, an inborn sense that words are really cool and that grammar is the coolest thing of all. Doing law is a great way to scratch that "do grammar" itch in the real world, solving problems of human beings.* Almost as much fun as studying linguistics and law as an academic researcher.

* And, OK, corporations and other institutions, but as a lawyer you get to choose your clients, if you're good. With linguistics in your background or as your love, why wouldn't you be?

Brief introduction to phonetics and phonology

Phonetics is about speech sounds, with two kinds of analysis, **articulatory** and **acoustic**. Articulatory phonetics describes speech sounds in terms of how they are produced – "articulated" – in the human mouth. Acoustic phonetics is about the sound waves speech produces. The little bit you'll need to know about acoustic phonetics is presented in Chapter 4. Here's a more detailed, though brief, introduction to articulatory phonetics:

Distinguishing vowels from consonants

Consonants are produced with obstruction in the vocal tract (basically the mouth): closure, as with **stops** (the airflow out is stopped) – [p t k b d g], [g] representing the "hard" sound as in *get* – or partial obstruction, as with **fricatives** (basically "friction noise" sounds) – [f v s z] and a few others, and with **nasals** (sounds made with the airflow going out the nose), like [m n ŋ] (the last representing the sound at the end of *song*).

Vowels are produced with no, or much less, obstruction. Depending on dialect, American English has eleven or 12 distinct vowel sounds, which might surprise you if you are bringing false assumptions about writing and spelling to your understanding of this material. As literate users of English we write five vowel letters, but there are lots more vowel sounds in English, as the list below shows. The symbols below the words are the phonetic symbols for the vowel sounds in the words above.

beat bit bait bet bat butt idea boot book broke caught cot.
[i] [ɪ] [e] [ɛ] [æ] [ʌ] [ə] [u] [ʊ] [o] [ɔ] [ɑ]

If you're a native of (basically) the western half of the U.S. you might find the vowel sounds of *caught* and *cot* the same. In your dialect of English, there are eleven distinct vowels; in eastern dialects there are twelve. Eastern speakers distinguish *cot* and *caught* by their vowel sounds, whereas for western speakers they're homonyms.

Voicing

All vowels and more than half the consonants of English are **voiced**, produced with vocal cord vibration. [v] is voiced, [f] voiceless. You can experience the difference by saying [ffff] and [vvvv] while holding a finger to your Adam's apple. You'll feel vibration with [v] and none with [f].

Phonetic transcription

Phonetic transcription is linguists' way of representing the sounds of any language. The good news is that lots of sounds are represented in the phonetic alphabet by familiar letters. [m] stands for the "m" sound, [b] for the "b" sound, [s] for the "s" sound. Here are most of the unfamiliar symbols used for English consonants: [ʃ ʒ θ ð tʃ dʒ]. These represent, respectively, the sounds of the underlined letters below, as shown in the full transcriptions of the words:

wash [wɑʃ] *measure* [mɛʒr̩] *ether* [iθr̩] *either* [iðr̩]
each [itʃ] *wedge* [wɛdʒ]

You can see that the sounds at the end of *each* and *wedge* are composite sounds. The little vertical line under the [r] in *measure*, *ether*, and *either* indicates a **syllabic** consonant, one that is vowel-like in forming the nucleus of a syllable. One other phonetic symbol to be aware of is [j], which represents the sound commonly spelled with the letter "y." So "yeast" is transcribed [jist].

You can be spared here the detailed description of how English consonants are articulated (go to any Linguistics One textbook if you want), but it'll be helpful to know about vowels. Vowels are distinguished articulatorily by four dimensions. **Height** is the position of the tongue, high, mid, or low: [mit] *meet*, [mɛt] *met*, [mæt] *mat*, respectively. The **front-back** dimension is where the body of the tongue most closely approaches the roof of the mouth: [i] *seen* (front), [u] *soon* (back). **Rounding** means forming the lips into something of a circle, as in [u] *soon* and [o] *sewn*. Finally, the **tense-lax** dimension distinguishes vowels produced with greater or less muscle tension. [i e u o] are tense; all other vowels are lax. *Beat* had the tense vowel [i]; *bit* has the lax vowel [ɪ].

Here's a chart of the English vowel sounds:

	Front	Central	Back
High	[i] [ɪ]		[u] [ʊ]
	meet mitt		*Luke look*
Mid	[e] [ɛ]	[ə] [ʌ]	[o] [ɔ]
	mate met	*idea luck*	*boat bought*
Low	[æ]	[a]	[ɑ]
	Mat		*hot*

English also has **diphthongs,** double vowels, as in *mine* [majn], *coin* [kɔjn], and *loud* [lawd]. The vowels in most American dialects in words like *mate* and *boat* are also diphthongs: [mejt, bowt].

The low central vowel [a] occurs in American English in the speech of native New Englanders, in words like *star* [staa], and in the speech of upper midwesterners (think Chicagoans) in words like *stop* [stap]. In the four pairs of sounds in the front and back columns, the first sound is tense, the second lax. The mid central vowels are distinguished by a fifth parameter (so I lied above when I said four, but this one is just for this pair of vowels): stress. [ʌ] is always stressed, as in *other* [ʌðr]; [ə] is always unstressed, as in *amend* [əmɛnd]. You can see the difference also in *above* [əbʌv], which has both [ə] and [ʌ].

Phonology

Speaking isn't just uttering the sounds of one's language in sequences that make up words. The sounds adjust to their position in a word or to the sounds around them in language-specific ways. For instance, English voiceless stop consonants [p t k] are **aspirated** word-initially, meaning produced with an [h]-like puff of breath. Compare the "p" sounds in *pill* and *spill* by pronouncing them normally while holding your palm a sixteenth of an inch in front of your lips. The puff you feel with the [p] in *pill* is **aspiration**, and it's absent from the [p] in *spill*. Aspirated sounds are represented in the phonetic alphabet by a little raised "h": [pʰɪl] *pill*. Unaspirated sounds are represented without it: [spɪl] *spill*. Most other languages don't have this **phonological rule**, Spanish, for example. (A great way to speak Spanish with an English accent is to aspirate the initial "p" in words like *pero* or *peso*.)

Speakers know the phonological rules for such sound adjustments unconsciously and apply them automatically. Generally, speakers don't even notice the adjustments, or that sounds subject to phonological rules are actually different.

Another English phonological rule lengthens (extends the duration of) vowels before voiced sounds. To experience this, say *leak* and *league*. The vowel in *league*, before the voiced [g], will be longer than the vowel in *leak*, which occurs before the voiceless [k]. Japanese doesn't have this rule. In fact, in Japanese, vowel length is sometimes the only phonetic difference between different words. Example: [biru] "building" – [biiru] "beer." When sounds are the only distinguishers between different words, the difference between the sounds is necessarily noticeable to native speakers of the language in question, though not necessarily for people learning that language if their native language has a different pattern for the same sounds (example: native English speakers learning Japanese). Sounds that can minimally distinguish words from each other in a language are called **phonemes**. Japanese [i] and [ii] are different phonemes in Japanese. In English, the same sounds are manifestations of *one* phoneme.

References

Ainsworth, Janet. 2011. The construction of admissions of fault through American rules of evidence: speech, silence, and significance in the legal creation of liability, in A. Wagner & L. Chen (eds), *Exploring Courtroom Discourse: the Language of Power and Control*. Ashgate Publishing/ Routledge: 177–192.

Brooks, Charles. 1966. Cartoon. *Birmingham News.* www.historytunes. com/images/cartoons/46-1.png (last visited Nov. 27, 2018).

Brown, Penelope, & Stephen Levinson. 1987. *Politeness: Some Universals in Language Usage.* Cambridge University Press.

Butters, Ronald. 2012. Linguistic analysis of disputed meanings: trademarks. *Encyclopedia of Applied Linguistics.*

Calabresi, Guido. 1982. *A Common Law for the Age of Statutes.* Harvard University Press.

Calabresi, Steven. Undated. White paper: Originalism in Constitutional interpretation. https://constitutioncenter.org/interactive-constitution/ white-pages/on-originalism-in-constitutional-interpretation

Calabresi, Steven, & Hannah Begley. 2016. Originalism and same-sex marriage. University of Miami Law Review 70: 648–707.

Chemerinksy, E. 2013. The inescapability of Constitutional theory. *University of Chicago Law Review* 80: 935–952.

Coleman, Linda, & Paul Kay. 1981. Prototype semantics: the English word *lie. Language* 57(1): 26–44.

Cunningham, Clark, & Charles Fillmore. 1995. Using common sense: a linguistic perspective on judicial interpretations of "use a firearm." *Washington University Law Review* 73(3): 1159–1214.

Eskridge, William. 1994. *Dynamic Statutory Interpretation.* Harvard University Press.

Eskridge, William, P. Frickey, & E. Garrett. 2007. *Legislation and Statutory Interpretation.* 2e. Foundation Press.

Frege, Gottlob. 1892. Über sinn und bedeutung. *Zeitschrift für Philosophie und philosophische Kritik,* vol. 100.

Fridman, G. 1956. Mens rea in conspiracy. *Modern Law Review* 19: 276–284.

Grice, Paul. 1957. Meaning. *The Philosophical Review* 66(3): 377–388.

Grice, Paul. 1975. Logic and conversation. In P. Cole & J. Morgan (eds), *Syntax and Semantics 3, Speech Acts.* Academic Press: 41–58.

Guy, Gregory. 2013. Current trends in sociolinguistics and applied linguistics: An interview with William Labov. *Calidoscópio* 11(1): 90–104.

Hart, H, & A. Sacks. 1958. The legal process: basic problems in the making and application of law (tent. ed.). Unpub. ms.

Kaplan, Jeffrey P. 2012. Unfaithful to textualism. *Georgetown Journal of Law and Public Policy* 10: 385–428.

Kaplan, Jeffrey P. 2016. Case report: *Elonis v. United States. International Journal of Speech, Language, and the Law* 23(2): 275–292.

Kersta, L. G. 1962. Voiceprint identification. *Nature* 196: 1253–1257.

Labov, William. 1988. The judicial testing of linguistic theory. In D. Tannen (ed), *Language in Context: Connecting Observation and Understanding.* Norwood: Ablex: 159–182.

Labov, William, Malcah Yeager, & Richard Steiner. 1972. *A Quantitative Study of Sound Change in Progress.* Report on National Science Foundation Contract NSF-GS-3287.

Leo, Richard. 2008. *Police Interrogation and American justice.* Harvard University Press.

Leo, Richard. & George Thomas (eds). 1998. *The Miranda Debate: Law, Justice, and Policing.* Northeastern University Press.

Lieber, Francis. 1839. *Legal and Political Hermeneutics, or Principles of Interpretation and Construction of Law and Politics with Remarks on Precedents and Authorities.* Little & Brown.

Llewellyn, Karl. 1950. Remarks on the theory of appellate decisions and the rules or canons about how statutes are to be construed. *Vanderbilt Law Review* 3: 395–406.

Morrison, Geoffrey. 2013. Introduction to logical reasoning for the evaluation of forensic evidence. BCIT – FSCT 7320 Introduction to Forensic Science. Guest Lecture.

New York Times. 1966. Miranda decision said to end effective use of confessions. August 21, 1966.

Peabody, B. 2016. Fifty years later, the Miranda decision hasn't accomplished what the Supreme Court intended. *Washington Post,* June 13, 2016.

Posner, R. 2012. The incoherence of Antonin Scalia. *The New Republic*, August 23, 2012. https://newrepublic.com/article/106441/scalia-garner-reading-the-law-textual-originalism

Prince, Ellen F. 1990. On the use of social conversation as evidence in a court of law. In Judith N. Levi & Anne Graffam Walker (eds), *Language in the Judicial Process*. Plenum Press: 279–289.

Rose, P. 2002. *Forensic Speaker Identification*. Taylor & Francis.

Scalia, Antonin. 1997. *A Matter of Interpretation*. Princeton University Press.

Scalia, Antonin, & Bryan Garner. 2012. *Reading Law: the Interpretation of Legal Texts*. Thomson West.

Schane, Sanford. 2012. Contract formation as a speech act, in Peter Tiersma & Lawrence Solan (eds), *The Oxford Handbook of Language and Law*. Oxford University Press: 100–113.

Searle, John. 1969. *Speech Acts. An Essay in the Philosophy of Language*. Cambridge University Press.

Searle, John. 1976. A classification of illocutionary acts. *Language in Society* 5(1): 1–23.

Shuy, Roger. 1997. Ten unanswered language questions about Miranda. *Forensic Linguistics* 4(2): 175–196.

Shuy, Roger. 2002. *Linguistic Battles in Trademark Disputes*. Palgrave MacMillan.

Shuy, Roger. 2011. Applied linguistics in the legal arena. In C. Candlin & S. Sarangi (eds), *Handbook of Communication in Organisations and Professions*. de Gruyter Mouton: 83–102.

Solan, Lawrence, & Peter Tiersma. 2005. *Speaking of Crime: the Language of Criminal Justice*. University of Chicago Press.

Sperber, Dan, & Dierdre Wilson. 1995. *Relevance: Communication and Cognition*. 2e. Blackwell.

Stevers, Alicia. 2017. Givenness and the said construction. Ms.

Strauss, D. 2010. *The Living Constitution*. Oxford University Press. Excerpt at https://www.law.uchicago.edu/news/living-constitution

Tiersma, Peter. 1987. The language of defamation. *Texas Law Review* 66: 303–350.

Tiersma, Peter. 1993. Nonverbal communication and the freedom of speech. *1993* Wisconsin Law Review: 1525–1589.

Tiersma, Peter. 1995. The ambiguity of interpretation: distinguishing interpretation from construction. Washington University Law Review 73(3): 1095–1101.

Tiersma, Peter. 2006 Some myths about legal language. *Journal of Law, Culture, and Humanities* 2(1): 29–50.

Tiersma, Peter. 2012. A history of the language of law. In P. Tiersma & L. Solan (eds), *The Oxford Handbook of Language and Law* 13–26: 19–26.

U.S. Department of Justice Criminal Resource Manual § 258. Admissibility of spectrograms (voice prints). https://www.justice.gov/jm/criminal-resource-manual-258-admissibility-spectrograms-voice-prints

Wrightsman, Lawrence S, & Mary L. Pitman. 2010. The Miranda ruling: its past, present, and future. Oxford University Press.

Cases

Adams v. Williams, 407 U.S. 143 (1972)

American Thermos Prod. Co. v. Aladdin Industries, Inc, 207 F. Supp. 9 (D. Conn. 1962)

Bailey v. United States, 516 U.S. 137 (1995)

Begay v. United States, 553 U.S. 137 (2008)

Berghuis v. Thompkins, 560 U.S. 370 (2010)

Bram v. United States, 168 U.S. 532 (1897)

Brewer v. Williams, 430 U.S. 387 (1977)

Bronston v. United States, 409 U.S. 352 (1973)

Brown v. Board of Education, 347 U.S. 483 (1954)

Brown v. Mississippi, 297 U.S. 278 (1936)

Brown v. State, 161 So. 165 (Miss. 1935).

Bumper v. North Carolina, 391 U.S. 543 (1968)

Chambers v. United States, 555 U.S. 122 (2009)

Circuit City Stores, Inc, v. Adams, 532 U.S. 105 (2001)

Colorado v. Connelly, 479 U.S. 157 (1986)

ConAgra v. Hormel, 990 F.2d 368 (1993).

District of Columbia v. Heller, 554 U.S. 570 (2008)

Daubert v. Merrell Dow Pharmaceuticals Inc, 509 U.S. 579 (1993)

Davis v. U.S, 512 U.S. 452 (1994)

Dickerson v. U.S, 530 U.S. 428 (2000)

Doyle v. Ohio, 426 U.S. 610 (1976)

Duckworth v. Eagan, 492 U.S. 195 (1989)

Eagan v. Duckworth, 843 F.2d 1554 (7th Cir.1988)

E.I. Du Pont de Nemours & Co. v. Yoshida Int'l, Inc, 393 F.Supp. 502 (E.D.N.Y, 1975)

Elliott v. Google, Inc, 860 F.3d 1151 (9th Cir. 2017).)

Elliott v. Google, 138 S.Ct. 362 (2017)

Elonis v. United States, 575 U.S.__(2015)

Escobedo v. Illinois, 378 U.S. 478 (1964)

Frye v. United States, 293 F. 1013 (D.C. Cir, 1923)

Gideon v. Wainwright, 372 U.S. 335 (1963)

Gilbert v. California, 388 U.S. 263 (1967).

Graham v. Florida, 560 U.S. 48 (2010)

Hamer v. Sidway, 124 N.Y. 538, 27 N.E. 256 (N.Y. 1891)

J. D. B. v. North Carolina, 564 U.S. 261 (2011)

James v. United States, 550 U.S. 192 (2007)

Jarecki v. G. D. Searle & Co, 367 U.S. 303 (1961)

Johnson v. U.S, 576 U.S. __, 135 S. Ct. 2551 (2015)

Keller v. Holderman, Mich. Sup. Ct, 11 Mich. 248 (1863)

Loving v. Virginia, 388 U.S. 1 (1967)

Lucas v. South Carolina Coastal Council, 505 U.S. 1003 (1992)).

Maryland v. Craig, 496 U.S. 836 (1990)

McDonald v. Chicago, 561 U.S. 742 (2010)

Michigan v. Long, 463 U.S. 1032 (1983)

Miranda v. Arizona, 384 U.S. 436 (1966)

Nelson v. Rice, 12 P.3E 238 (Ariz. App. 2000)

North Carolina v. Butler, 441 U.S. 369 (1979)

Obergefell v. Hodges, 576 U.S. ___ (2015

Pacific Gas & Electric Co. v. G.W. Thomas Drayage and Rigging Co, 442 P.2d 641 (Cal. 1968).

Pennsylvania v. Mimms, 434 U.S. 106 (1977)

Pennsylvania v. Muniz, 496 U.S. 582 (1990)

People v. Gordon, 47 Cal. App. 3d 465 (1975)

Playtex Products v. Georgia-Pacific Corporation and Fort James Operating Corp, 390 F.3d 158 (2d Cir. 2004)

Raffles v Wichelhaus 2 H. & C. 906, 159 Eng. Rep. 373 (Ex. 1864)

Rector, etc, of Holy Trinity Church v. U.S, 143 U.S. 457 (1892)

Rhode Island v. Innis, 446 U.S. 291 (1980)

Rogers v. Richmond, 365 U.S. 534 (1961

Salinas v. Texas, 570 U.S. (2013)

Schmerber v. California, 384 U.S.757 (1966)

Schneckloth v. Bustamonte, 412 U.S. 218 (1973)

Sherwood v. Walker, 33 N.W. 919 (Mich. 1887)

Smith v. U.S, 508 U.S. 223 (1993)

Spano v. New York, 360 U.S. 315 (1959)

Sykes v. United States, 564 U.S. 1 (2011)

Terry v. Ohio, 392 U.S. 1 (1968)

Texas v. Johnson, 491 U.S. 397 (1989)

Townsend v. Sain, 372 U.S. 293 (1963)

Trop v. Dulles, 356 U.S. 86 (1958)

U.S. v. Angleton, 269 F. Supp. 2d 892 (S.D. Tex. 2003

U.S. v. Hale, 422 U.S 171, 176 (1975)

U.S. v. Wade, 388 U.S. 218 (1967)

U.S. v. X-Citement Video, 513 U.S. 64 (1994),

U.S. v. Yermian, 468 U.S. 63 (1984).

Watkins & Sons v. Carrig, 21 A.2d 591 (N.H. 1941)

Wood v. Boynton, Wisc. Sup. Ct,, 25 N.W. 42 (1885)

Index

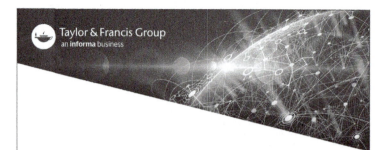

77450649R00134